'Louwerse reveals how surprisingly similar [...] into a human mind and that of peering i[...] thus why cognitive psychology has much [...]'

**Max S. Bennett,** *author of A Brief History of Intelligence*

'This is a very accessible and readable book for anyone interested in AI. The author's way of providing real world simple examples makes it easy to relate to the subject matter often by considering everyday life.'

**Kevin Warwick,** *professor at Coventry and Reading Universities, UK, and author of six popular science books on AI and cybernetics*

'This book explains the tight relationship between AI and cognitive psychology since the beginning of AI 70 years ago. Ray Kurtzweil and Yuval Noah Harari have been helping the public understand the past and future of AI. Max Louwerse has written a very engaging and readable book for the public to understand how psychological science can explain many of the mysteries of AI.'

**Art Graesser,** *professor at the University of Memphis, USA and Honorary Research Fellow at the University of Oxford, UK*

To my parents, John and Suzan Louwerse,
and of course to Desirée, Quinten and Eleane

# CONTENTS

# WHO AM I AND WHY AM I GIVING YOU THIS ADVICE?

Think about this for a second or two. You are seeing these wiggly shapes in front of you and are miraculously creating meaning out of them. Or you are hearing bursts of sounds coming out of somebody's mouth and are able to understand what it is that person is telling you. This transformation of symbols into meaning is an amazing accomplishment that each one of us have started to master the moment we were born. The question how language attains meaning has always fascinated me. It is one important piece of the puzzle how the human mind works. And one way to understand how the human mind works (and how language attains meaning) is to build mechanisms of the human mind in an artificial mind.

The topic of this book is one close to my heart, and particularly my academic heart. As a PhD candidate in Psycholinguistics and Computational Linguistics at the University of Edinburgh in Scotland, I had the opportunity to study how humans understand text, and how we can build computer models that mimic the cognitive mechanisms. Driven by curiosity, I ran response time and eye tracking experiments with human participants, and developed computer models that simulated these findings.

Following my PhD I was fortunate enough to land a professorship at the University of Memphis in the United States, home of a conversational intelligent tutoring system that had discussions with students on a variety of topics, from conceptual physics to computer literacy. It was able to understand students through conversations and provide a personalized learning experience. This intelligent tutoring system was built after human tutors, after human minds. And that artificial mind in turn provided exciting perspectives on the human mind.

Some of my colleagues argued (and still argue) that artificial minds can never be intelligent. That they could never understand language, because a machine simply does not have a human mind. Sure, machines do not have a human brain. *That* we can definitely agree on. The question however is whether the mechanisms of human and artificial minds show similarities. With regards to extracting meaning of language I have argued that much of the magic of creating meaning actually lies in the language system itself. It is up to human and artificial minds to pick up these patterns. With my research lab we ran studies showing how meaning can be extracted from language. We predicted the findings of experimental studies that demonstrated how language users activated perceptual simulations by only using language patterns. We conducted studies on predicting the longitude and latitude of locations in Middle Earth only by computing how location names appeared in *Lord of the Rings*. Similarly, we ran studies helping archaeologists with excavation sites using simple patterns in the Indus script.

Later, back on the other side of the Big Pond, as a Professor in Cognitive Psychology and Artificial Intelligence at Tilburg University and Professor by Special Appointment at Maastricht University in the Netherlands, I have continued trying to understand artificial minds by studying the human mind, and understand human minds by building artificial ones. Driven by the same curiosity from years ago, we have created a computer system that analyses text across hundreds of dimensions for over 40 languages. Meanwhile I am directing a large virtual reality lab where immersive education and training take place while people are interacting with each other and the virtual world. These interactive virtual reality simulations are projected in a 360° environment while 44 loudspeakers behind the walls add to the immersive experience. Exciting research on innovations in education!

I am collaborating on projects where we are using augmented reality to let surgeons see through a patient during surgery. With an augmented reality headset, they can perform their surgical procedures – from neurosurgery to vascular surgery – while seeing the inside of the patient, reducing 20 minutes of preparatory surgery time to only 10 seconds.

We are running projects where we build brain-computer interfaces to provide pilots with personalized flight simulation, providing a feedback loop between their neurophysiological behaviour and the virtual reality simulation.

We are conducting research projects where we create virtual humans in a virtual world that look and behave exactly like their human copy. A digital twin that can be used as an intelligent tutoring system, guiding learners through interactive learning material.

And I am helping to launch tens of thousands of children across the world into space. As part of an international educational program driven by the non-profit organisation SpaceBuzz, children are part of an astronaut training that results in an actual rocket ship arriving in front of their school, ready to become ambassadors of planet Earth. Seated in their rocket seats, they are launched into space, orbiting the Earth. And no worries, this is all part of a virtual reality experience.

I guess I am a hungry scientist in the candy store called "Psychology and AI". That's probably why I have always loved popular science as a reader. But I have also learned to love popular science as an author, as exemplified by my popular science book *Keeping those Words in Mind: How Language Creates Meaning*, my blogging for *Psychology Today*, and the talks I give to both academic but also non-academic audiences. I hope the book you are now reading reflects that love. I truly hope this book allows me to instil a bit of the curiosity, excitement, and enthusiasm I myself have for the topic of cognitive psychology and artificial intelligence onto *you*, the reader, and let you be part of the journey of understanding human and artificial minds.

# PREFACE

Artificial intelligence is hot. There is no sign the excitement about its opportunities and the unrest about its threats will be cooling down any time soon. The latest accomplishments of yet another state-of-the-art AI breakthrough will simply be even more mind blowing, regardless of whether these accomplishments are hyped by the industry or the media. There is excitement about the prospects AI has to offer when it comes to curing diseases, predicting disasters, and making life more enjoyable by taking over the tasks that we all would least like to do. There is excitement about the thinking power AI displays, as well as its creativity when producing poetry and prose, pictures and paintings, cartoons, movies and music. Meanwhile there is also fear in society, fear that AI will be smarter than us, will take over our jobs, that it will govern our lives, or that it will even take over mankind altogether. It is therefore no wonder there is so much to read about AI on social media, in the news, and in publications. Indeed, there really is no shortage of outstanding popular science books written on AI. Why would one then want to read yet another book on AI? The answer is simple and has everything to do with how AI is perceived by many.

Paraphrasing a popular quote used for data science a decade ago, artificial intelligence is like teenage sex: everyone talks about it, everyone knows they will be involved in it at some point, everyone thinks everyone else is doing it, many are primarily concerned with performance, many warn about the risks of doing it unprotected, and yet too many others do not really know what it entails. And particularly that last group of people is a concern: not knowing what it entails and yet knowing you will be involved in it at some point brings challenges, and might be the very reason for unrest and fear. Perhaps less so for teenage sex, but certainly for AI.

When the British Psychological Society contacted me about an accessible introduction to AI, I hesitated. My love for writing a popular science book had certainly not diminished since my last book on language, cognition, and computation. But there are already so many books on AI, that I wondered what I could add. I asked around what AI meant to others, not so much querying my colleagues in AI, but my friends and family. And I realized that for many of us AI is a dark black box of magic, with increasing amounts of magic being poured out over our society. Amazing magic, but very much a black box. For many of us asking what AI entails today may start to feel increasingly embarrassing, simply because AI seems to have become so ubiquitous. No matter the depth and insights in popular science books on AI currently out there, these are hardly any *simple* introductions, let alone introductions into the multifaceted aspects of AI and its mechanisms. This book is written to make a difference.

Each chapter will start with an introduction on a topic from the field of psychology, and will then move to the field of AI. That is, a chapter will start out with understanding a topic from the perspective of human minds, meant to benefit the second part of a chapter from the perspective of artificial minds. Consequently, what is covered in the psychology section serves as a background for the AI section.

A simple and accessible introduction to AI runs the risk of being oversimplistic. For the book you are currently reading some may argue that important topics are missing, that the discussion of covered topics is too basic, that the examples and analogies do not do justice to the heart of the issue, and that describing the field of AI in only two hundred pages is way too concise given that others need well over a thousand pages. And those critics are right. And yet, I think there does seem to be a need for a simple introduction. While information about AI, and applications using AI, are skyrocketing, many of us steer away from AI because they think they already missed the boat. This book is also for the reader entirely unfamiliar with very idea of AI.

This book is however not only about AI. It is about AI from the perspective of psychology. There are many reasons why the disciplines of psychology and AI have had very close ties. We will come to those. Today's researchers in AI may argue that historically AI and psychology were once perhaps happily married, but recently AI got into a divorce and started its own life independent from psychology. Because of its independence, this new AI would hardly benefit from insights from psychology, one might argue. This may be true to an extent, but it would then still be worthwhile to understand artificial minds from an understanding of human minds, separate from the discussion to what extent AI is dependent on psychological insights. I would however argue that the strong ties between psychology and AI have been there and likely remain to be there. My argument would be that we may understand artificial minds best through an understanding of human minds and vice versa.

Given the conciseness of this book and its introductory nature I will not discuss specific programming languages, detailed algorithms, machine learning models, or the latest applications. These can be found elsewhere. Instead, I aim to discuss artificial minds from the perspective of human minds, and vice versa. If you are new to AI and are looking for a non-expert introduction, or if you are interested in the human mind and the similarities and differences with its computational counterpart, this may be the right book for you. But if you are simply interested in a readable introduction on how human and artificial minds relate, this would certainly be the book to read.

A big thank you to Rachel Sangster and the British Psychological Society for inviting me to me to write this book. Also, a big thanks to Annabelle Harris, Ceri McLardy, Tori Sharpe, and Shivran-jani Singh, Leah Kinthaert, and Curtis Hill from Taylor and Francis and Routledge for making this exciting project possible, and Judit Varga for proofreading the manuscript. A very (very!) big thank you to friends and colleagues Eric Postma, Frank Hakemulder, and Guido Linders, who were willing to courageously read drafts of this book. Of course, the many thoughtful corrections are theirs, the remaining thoughtless mistakes are mine.

# 1

## HOW DO HUMAN AND ARTIFICIAL MINDS RELATE?

*Will artificial intelligence become more intelligent than human intelligence?* This question keeps popping up in the media. Frankly, I have never quite understood the question, let alone found an answer to it. But I do think I know where the question comes from. And that is the very reason for writing a book on the psychology of artificial intelligence, on human and artificial minds. This book takes what we know about the human mind, our own mind, in order to learn about artificial minds. Moreover, in the endeavour of understanding artificial minds, we may in fact learn a thing or two about the human mind. But why relate human and artificial minds?[1]

### HUMAN MINDS?

Let's start out with human minds before we move to artificial minds. Psychology studies the brain, the mind and behaviour. The brain is the organ that serves as the centre of the nervous system in most animals[2]. Identifying the brain and the nervous system in humans and non-humans is relatively easy. We pretty much know its location, and we can measure its activity using various brain imaging devices. By no means does this mean that we fully understand the brain or that such understanding is easy, but at least we know where to identify

DOI: 10.4324/9781003491095-1

the nervous system and the brain in most species[3]. In case we were to struggle to find it, we can look for organs for special senses such as vision, hearing and olfaction. The brain is pretty much located closest to them.

Whereas identifying the location of the brain is straightforward, identifying the location of the mind turns out to be a major challenge. We don't really know what the mind is. Sure, it is the totality of psychological phenomena, as a textbook in psychological science would state. But that does not make things very concrete. Perhaps stated plainly, the mind is what the brain does[4]. Indeed, stated simply.

For many centuries the relation between the mind and the brain has been a hot topic of debate. Already in Ancient Greece philosophers Plato and Aristotle wondered about the relationship of the soul and the physical body, and asked the question whether the mind is a physical entity or something else, and whether the mind controls the body. These mind-body questions became most prominent in the 17th century when French philosopher René Descartes identified the mind as an entity with consciousness and self-awareness, and distinguished it from the brain as the seat of intelligence. This dualist perspective has waned over the years, but the nature of the relationship between the brain and the mind has continued being under discussion in a variety of disciplines, from philosophy to psychology, from psychology to artificial intelligence. It is an interesting discussion for the psychology of artificial intelligence. Some argue that the mind is reducible to physical processes. To them, the mind is not much more than the physical processes in the brain. Others have argued that the physical world is entirely dependent on the mind. So much so that there is no physical world without the mind. If nobody can see or hear it, it basically does not exist. Some even argue that there is an extended mind in the physical world that our human mind takes advantage of. Objects that store information for us, helping our own cognitive processes. The notes we take, the scribbles we make, but also the laptops and mobile phones we use[5].

The mind-body problem, or the mind-matter problem as it has been called, or actually the mind-brain problem as it can be called, is critical in understanding human minds and artificial minds. After all, it seeks answers to the relationship between mental phenomena such as thoughts, feelings, and consciousness, and physical phenomena, such as brain processes and bodily functions. Gaining insight into the relationship between brain and mind might help us gain insight in what is still one of the mysterious aspects of our very existence. But such insights would also help us understand how the brain produces mental states. And it would shed light on artificial intelligence. Not only in the development of artificial intelligence and robotics, but also in the debate on whether machines can have minds. Or consciousness. Or emotions. And as a consequence, how to ethically treat these intelligent systems.

Now if the mind is what the brain does, we could simply extrapolate that behaviour is what the mind does. The cognitive process in our mind of figuring out the solution of solving a puzzle guides our behaviour in arranging the pieces. The mental emotion of being scared might trigger our behaviour of fighting against the threat or running away from it. And our mental state of feeling hungry might propel our behaviour to seek food. Behaviour can thus be seen as the outward manifestation of the mind's inner processes.

## ARTIFICIAL MINDS?

If psychology is the study of brain, mind and behaviour, what then is artificial intelligence? The field of artificial Intelligence may be seen as the field of computational psychology or psychological engineering. Now, even if you are convinced that AI is computer science instead of psychology, just bear with me. Analogously to the definition of psychology, artificial Intelligence is the study of the hardware, the software, and its actions. The study of the computer, the artificial mind and its output.

The metaphorical brain of artificial minds is the computer. These can be the general-purpose computers you are likely most familiar with, the desktop and laptop computers. But they also include servers; powerful computers that provide services and manage network resources for other computers, mainframes and supercomputers; the high-performance systems used for large-scale computing tasks, such as scientific simulations and complex data processing, and embedded systems; specialized computers integrated into other devices. The brain of the computer is the Central Processing Unit, the CPU. It is responsible for executing instructions and processing data. Of course, in addition, other components of the hardware can be identified such as the temporary storage that holds data and instructions that the CPU needs while performing tasks (RAM), the permanent storage for data and programs (hard drives). Just like the human brain, computers take quite some energy. If we assume that a computer powered by 100 watts is used for 24 hours, it will consume 2.4 kilowatt-hours of energy. However, if we move away from your PC, energy consumption for a query in ChatGPT is approximately 6.79 watt-hour. About 350 ChatGPT queries per day make up the energy consumption of the human brain. For a more energy efficient DeepSeek that number of queries lies about 10 times higher. But it is likely that throughout the day (and night) you make far more metaphorical queries in your mind when processing the world around you, thinking your thoughts and dreaming your dreams.

The metaphorical mind of what the computer does is the software. Just like the mind is what the brain does, software is what the hardware does. Software concerns the instructions and programs that tell the hardware what to do. Just like brain activity gives rise to mental processes, the computer hardware requires software to perform its tasks. Without a mind the brain is inert, without software hardware is. Without a brain, there is no mind as we understand it. Without a computer, there is no software as we understand it. Software needs hardware to run; it cannot execute on its own. Human minds need human brains. Artificial minds need artificial brains.

Whereas the mind-brain relationship is extremely complex, the software-hardware relationship is quite well understood. In part this has to do with the fact that the analogy of the brain-mind and hardware-software is not perfect. For instance, concepts such as consciousness and subjective experience are far from being understood, for they concern aspects that are not comparable to software operations. When it comes to the human hardware and software, we know that a range of biological, psychological, and environmental factors influence their operations: Genetic factors, socio-economic background, and psychological disorders have a major impact on our cognitive processes. Software, on the other hand, follows more predictable instructions provided by code.

At the same time, what we may consider straightforward now in our understanding of hardware and software could easily become as complex as the mind-brain problem. For instance, current computers operate on a stream of electrical impulses in a binary manner. They operate on 1s and 0s. Quantum computers, instead, use quantum bits, or qubits, seemingly existing in more than one state (i.e., 1 and 0) at the same time. They are therefore expected to be exponentially faster than a classical computer. That means that a problem that may take millions of years to compute on a classical computer, a powerful quantum computer may find the solution for in hours or even minutes. In other words, we may understand computers so well, because their current implementations are so simple. Software is often seen in terms of algorithms, finite sequences of mathematically rigorous instructions to solve a class of specific problems or to perform a computation. But what if the finite sequences we are so familiar with in computers were to become infinite? What if the software we tend to think of as being controlled by humans starts to write itself, so that humans have no longer insight in the nature of the very code that is executed? What if the code evolves into a system that only machines themselves understand and these autonomous machines develop consciousness? Imagine humans can no longer intervene in the decisions these intelligent machines make. The consequences might spiral out of control.

In the analogy between brain, mind and behaviour in humans (psychology) and computers (artificial intelligence), and in the analogies between human and artificial minds, I should hasten to say that not all definitions in AI focus on making machines think and learn like humans or on creating AI systems that mimic human cognitive processes. Other definitions focus on AI as the ability of a machine to simulate human behaviour or actions, regardless of whether its mechanisms show any similarity[6]. One could develop algorithms and statistical models to enable computer systems that can recognize pictures, or avoid obstacles when driving, irrelevant whether or not computational processes are humanlike. According to such definitions the focus of AI relies on machine learning irrespective of human learning.

For the sake of discussion in this book, I follow the idea that artificial intelligence focuses on artificial minds which are analogous to human minds. I do not do this because it is necessarily the only definition, but because that definition helps us to understand the similarities and differences between human minds and artificial minds. That is, even if by the end of this book one were to conclude that there currently is no longer a necessary analogy between the two, explaining artificial minds by human minds helps us understand issues in artificial intelligence and psychology alike. And there are quite some reasons to consider a psychology of artificial intelligence, including historical, terminological and conceptual reasons.

## HOW TO RELATE HUMAN AND ARTIFICIAL MINDS HISTORICALLY?

When following the media, it is almost as if AI was recently invented and took us by surprise invading the very roots of our society. So much so that artificial intelligence has now been awarded with a determiner: we often speak of the artificial intelligence. And yet AI is not at all a recent phenomenon. It has a very rich history.

Our fascination with artificial minds is thousands of years old. Homer's *Iliad* and *Odyssey* are commonly not seen as works of science fiction that provide us with an insight into the future of intelligent systems. Yet almost 3,000 years ago, Homer described the machines that we now envision when thinking of artificial intelligence. In Homer's *Iliad*, for instance, artificial intelligence is described in young robots that look like women and know what to do by themselves. It is Hephaistos, god of fire, smiths, craftsmen, metalworking, stone-masonry and sculpture, who is the creator of these automatons, these self-operating machines acting like humans. And it is not just in the *Iliad* that Homer rolls out these initial ideas of artificial-intelligence controlled entities, these artificial minds. In the *Odyssey* too, Homer speaks of AI-operated ships. Artificial intelligence 3,000 years *avant la lettre*.

Perhaps more concretely the history of artificial intelligence can be traced back 1,200 years when Persian scientist Muḥammad ibn Mūsā al-Khwārizmī wrote the book that translates to *The Compendious Book on Calculation by Completion and Balancing*. One of the words in the original Arabic title, الجبر or "al-jabr", is the origin of our current word for algebra. And the author's name (al-Khwārizmī) is the origin of our current word for algorithm, what we now know in computer science and artificial intelligence as the sequence of instructions used to perform a computation. And the very idea of a computer has also been around for a while, originally finding its source in the Latin *putare* which means both "to think" and "to prune". Over the years we have been doing quite some thinking and pruning, as a "computer" used to be a person who did calculations. In fact, in 1731 the Edinburgh Weekly Journal advised young married women to know their husbands' income "and be so good a Computer as to keep within it."[7]

Generally, however, the history of AI is traced back to the 19th century, to Ada Lovelace, daughter of poet Lord Byron, who expressed a desire to create a mathematical model for how the brain gives rise to thoughts, and nerves to feelings. She proposed a calculus of the nervous system, and perhaps she should be seen as the founder of AI, as some would argue. At the same time, Ada Lovelace also stated that AI engines have no capacity whatsoever to originate anything and can only do whatever we tell them to do. But the very idea of AI is exactly that it can develop in ways that cannot necessarily be anticipated by programmers. . .

Regardless of whether artificial intelligence goes back thousands of years, hundreds of years, or only a few decades, there is one very specific date that officially launched artificial intelligence, at least its name. In the summer of 1956, a workshop in Dartmouth was attended by a group of computer scientists. These computer scientists were all interdisciplinary. They worked in computer science as well as another field of research, such as mathematics, engineering or physics. But most of the computer scientists shared an interest with one specific field, that of psychology. Of the group who attended the workshop, approximately half were professors of computer science and psychology. One of these professors was the organizer of the workshop himself, John McCarthy, who coined the term "artificial intelligence".

In actual fact, artificial intelligence was born in a project proposal to the Rockefeller Foundation requesting funding for the summer seminar at Dartmouth. The seminar would be held

> to proceed on the basis of the conjecture that every aspect of learning or any other feature of intelligence can in principle be so precisely described that a machine can be made to simulate it. An attempt [would] be made to find how to make machines use language, form abstractions and concepts, solve kinds of problems now reserved for humans, and improve themselves.[8]

Topics that were discussed during these summer months in 1956 included how computers can simulate humans, how computers can use human language, how computers can form concepts and how they can improve as intelligent machines and become more efficient. All presentations focused on computational implementations, or questions regarding such computational implementations, of human skills and expertise.

The Dartmouth workshop as the formal inception of artificial intelligence can be found in practically any book that describes the history of artificial intelligence. The fact that all who attended the workshop were *interdisciplinary* scholars generally does not receive much attention, and the fact that half of the attendees were *psychologists* receives even less attention. That these scientists were very interdisciplinary, however, explains the excitement about thinking machines. The Dartmouth workshop that coined the term artificial intelligence was pretty much trying to find computational answers to psychology questions.

What often does not get mentioned either in descriptions of the history on artificial intelligence is an event that also explains the major breakthrough of artificial intelligence in the 1950s. A few months after the Dartmouth workshop a symposium was organized by the "Special Interest Group in Information Theory" at the Massachusetts Institute of Technology. This symposium had a major impact on psychology for it launched "the cognitive revolution". Since the early 1900s psychology used to be considered as the science of behaviour. Behaviour, according to the leading psychologists at the time, was induced by external events[9]. A dog salivates after hearing a bell, when the dog associates the presence of the external stimulus of meat with the external stimulus of ringing of a bell. Rats learn how to press a lever after the external stimulus of receiving food as a reward to increase the behaviour of pressing a lever or decreasing that behaviour when receiving the external stimulus of an electrical shock. To the common psychology view at the time, human behaviour, just like all animal behaviour, was considered a response to stimuli. Mental events did not belong to psychology because they were not observable behaviour, according to the leading behaviourist view. Memory could not be observed, only observable learning could. Language processing in the mind could not be observed, so language processing became verbal behaviour in response to positive and negative feedback. The mind was not observable, and therefore scientists ought to instead focus on what the mind does, its behaviour. The fact that we are able to think many thoughts without any stimuli was interesting according to behaviourists, but not observable and therefore not important.

The MIT workshop in 1956 overturned the idea that only behaviour rather than the mind should be studied. At the MIT workshop, papers were presented on the mathematical study of the quantification and communication of information, on analysing, modifying and synthesizing signals, and on the mathematical structure of language. The move away from stimulus and the response towards cognition, gave rise to what has been dubbed the "cognitive revolution". Just like the excitement for computers that can think propelled the field of AI, the excitement surrounding the cognitive revolution propelled "information-processing psychology" ultimately becoming to be known as the field of "cognitive science". And just like the Dartmouth workshop was trying to find a computational answer to psychology questions (from a computer science perspective), the MIT workshop was trying to do the same (from a psychology perspective).

The topics at both the Dartmouth and MIT workshops were very similar, and both workshops were attended by several of the very same researchers, including psychologist and Nobel Prize winner Herb Simon and computer scientists and cognitive psychologist Allen Newell. Cognitive psychologist George Miller later wrote:

> I left the symposium with a conviction, more intuitive than rational, that experimental psychology, theoretical linguistics, and the computer simulation of cognitive processes were all pieces from a larger whole and that the future would see a progressive elaboration and coordination of their shared concerns.[10]

Miller could not have been more right.

The cognitive revolution and the launch of artificial intelligence both in 1956 is not coincidental of course. In the early to mid 1950s the early days of commercial computers had arrived. On March 8, 1955, MIT introduced the Whirlwind machine, a revolutionary computer that was the first digital computer with magnetic core RAM (random-access memory) and real-time graphics. The enthusiasm about, and promise of, the thinking powers of computers created a new field (artificial intelligence) and redefined others (cognitive science). Computers became the vehicle to develop artificial minds, and human minds served as a perfect example.

## HOW TO RELATE HUMAN AND ARTIFICIAL MINDS TERMINOLOGICALLY?

No matter how much one *may* want to juxtapose psychology and AI, the two have become inseparable. No matter how one *may* want to leave their historical roots aside, AI is bound to psychology. This is most obvious in the very name "artificial intelligence": half of the name borrowed from the very psychological concept. But the borrowing of terminology does not stop there. There is a large range of terms in artificial intelligence that are borrowed from psychology. As we will see throughout this book, terms so common to the field of AI, from "training" to "testing", from artificial "neural networks" to "learning", from "reinforcement" to "performance", from "biases" to "predictions", artificial intelligence generously borrows from psychology[11]. It is hard to find a concept in artificial intelligence that is not reminiscent of the psychological roots for that concept.

The dependence of AI on psychology is not a surprise. When it comes to thinking machines, we are of course very much constrained by our own thinking. Paraphrasing psychologist Abraham Maslow: "It is tempting, if the only tool you have is a hammer, to treat everything as if it were a nail."[12] If the only tool we have is the human mind, we likely treat any computational simulation from a psychological perspective. We are simply bound by our human cognitive constraints and terminology to think about artificial minds. What's more, humans excel at anthropomorphizing. They attribute human characteristics, behaviours, or emotions to non-human entities, such as animals, objects, or natural phenomena. When we see our dog looking sad and our cat looking happy, we ignore the fact that animals often do not express emotions in the same way humans do. Meanwhile we yell at our computer when it does not work, even though the machine does not listen and will not work any better with some yelling. We just cannot stop attributing human characteristics to machines that seem to think.

## HOW TO RELATE HUMAN AND ARTIFICIAL MINDS CONCEPTUALLY?

Textbooks that serve as introductions to psychology often pose the question how we can learn about the black box, called the mind. They provide three answers to this question.

One answer is to pry open the black box. We carefully look inside the black box, and try to understand how it is wired and how signals travel through these (metaphorical) wires. We can either literally pry open the box we call the brain, and place receptors on the (metaphorical) wires, or place receptors on the outside of the black box to measure activity of the (metaphorical) wires. Neuroscience uses both approaches.

Another answer is to measure the behaviour produced by the black box. We can ask the organism to perform a particular task, and measure its performance on that task to gather insights in the mental processes. For instance, we could measure response times on a particular task to determine how quickly a participant reaches a decision. Or we can monitor a participant's eye gaze and try to gain insight in reading processes based on what a reader pays attention to. Cognitive psychology takes this approach. How the brain does it is less relevant, how the mind does it instead is the central question.

Finally, there is a third answer how to learn about the black box (the brain) and what it does (the mind): We can re-build the black box ourselves. Once we have such a black box, we now have the opportunity to simulate what goes on. And this has a range of advantages. First of all, we can run thousands of simulations on our artificial mind and see what happens when these simulations undergo different manipulations. Second, we can handicap the system and gather insights in what would happen if the black box does not function the way it should. And finally, we can pry the box open and measure the behaviour of what the box does, feed that in our artificial mind, and test for new hypotheses. Both cognitive psychology and cognitive neuroscience develop computational models of the brain and mind. But artificial intelligence particularly does so.

Today's artificial intelligence is less about the human mind than about building sophisticated computer models that may or may not be related to the human cognitive version. Perhaps in 1956 the human mind was considered to be computational, and computers may seem to simulate human cognitive processes, today's psychology and AI would view this differently. Current AI models may even surpass the performance, capacity and processes of the human mind. One may argue that the artificial intelligence of today is not concerned anymore with flying by building flapping wings modelled after a bird, as it is with building entire airplanes itself that have very little to do with bird flight. Planes and birds both fly, but this is where the similarity pretty much ends. But even if one were to take the stance that the field of AI has moved well beyond what the field of psychology can contribute, I would hasten to say we can still learn a lot from psychology.

Likewise, today's psychologists may argue that the human mind should definitely not be seen as a computer. For instance, for them, the human mind should not be seen in isolation, but in combination with the human body, and bodies computers simply lack. A computer will fundamentally fail in considering embodied cognition. Here too, even if one were to take the stance that psychology should not look at the human mind from a computational perspective, I would again hasten to say that we learned a lot about the human mind from the computational metaphor, so much so that the discussion on an embodied mind would not have taken place had the similarity between the human mind and a computational mind not been made.

An additional reason to consider AI from a psychological perspective comes from the common concern in AI these days that the computational models it uses are black boxes. It is very difficult to understand how complex AI models reach their conclusions. The field of Explainable AI tries to fix this problem by building algorithms that reveal the mechanisms that underlie the decision the algorithm comes up with. At a theoretical level these mechanisms may also be explained by psychological mechanisms, even if they are not necessarily the actual psychological mechanisms in the human mind, they at least are an attempt to explain mechanisms somehow with the human mind.

Finally, there is another, very pragmatic reason too for considering artificial intelligence from a psychological perspective, and that reason perhaps touches most on the aim of this book. Readers unfamiliar with the field of artificial intelligence can be introduced to algorithms, formulas and applications. But an introduction into artificial minds is perhaps easiest to follow from an understanding of the human mind. It may be easier to start out with what we know about the human mind and project it onto artificial minds. After all, with our own mental machinery we don't really have much of a choice.

## HOW TO RELATE APPLES AND ORANGES?

But wait, wait, you might say. Historical, terminological and conceptual reasons aside, the mind is what the brain does. AI does not have a brain. We could metaphorically describe a computer as an artificial brain, but really AI does not have a brain. If we move beyond a metaphorical comparison, a silicon computer is very different from a brain, so at best one can make a comparison at a very abstract level. One where apples and oranges are compared because they both happen to be fruits. This is an important issue. Very often the conclusion that findings in psychology and AI cannot be compared stems from a confusion that comes from comparing different levels of analyses[13]. This confusion has become so fundamental in understanding human and artificial minds, that it is worth explaining it in more detail along the ideas of neuroscientist and physiologist David Marr who integrated results from psychology, artificial intelligence, and neurophysiology.

Let's take the game of football as an example to understand these different levels of analysis. At one level "what" and "why" questions are answered. Let's call this the *rational* level. At the rational level the question gets answered what the fundamental purpose is of the game of football. The answer at this level is that the purpose of football is to get a ball across the field to score. Keep in mind that the question *how* this is done is irrelevant for this level. Instead, the rational level focuses on the nature of the problem that needs to be solved.

At a different level are questions of *how* information is processed and what steps are involved to score. Let's call this the *information processing* level. Here the question gets asked, what procedures and rules are followed to achieve the goal of scoring? For instance, how is the ball kicked across the field to score? After all, when a ball is kicked across the field, it may lead to scoring, but there are also other means to score (albeit kicking the ball across the field seems the best method). The information processing level is not so much concerned with the *problem*, the purpose of scoring, but with the *process* itself. The question at the information level focuses on the strategies, how the computation of scoring a goal is performed.

Finally, there is a third level where we are not so much concerned with the problem, the purpose of the game of football, or the strategies used to score, but where questions are answered regarding the medium, the using of one's left foot and right foot. Let's call this the *biological* level. At this level, the physical system comes into play, the physical processes how the steps are executed.

Studying the complex system of football by only studying the actions of the right foot (*biological level*), or by exclusively focusing on the trajectory of getting the ball across the field (*information processing level*), or by exclusively looking at the scoring (*rational level*), does not do justice to the complexity of the system. Instead, we ought to consider the differences across these levels: the why (the problem), the what (the rules) and the how (the physical system). What the system aims to do, how the system does what it does and what the physical hardware of the system is are three very different things.

Distinguishing between these three levels is important for understanding human minds, artificial minds, and for understanding the relation between them. Let's start with the human mind. When neuroscientists explain where in the brain particular processes have taken place, this undoubtedly leads to very valuable insights. Understanding the brain regions, the neural circuits, and neurotransmitter systems involved in cognitive functions help us to address questions related to the biological and neural underpinnings of cognitive processes. However, it would be unfair to accuse neuroscientists that, by studying the brain, they do not explain *how* cognitive processes are carried out and what mental strategies are employed. After all, that question concerns a different level of analysis. Now, cognitive psychologists may study specific algorithms and processes that the cognitive system uses to achieve its goals. For instance, they may ask participants to participate in an experiment to get insights into how fast participants process different kinds of stimuli. But it would be unfair to accuse these cognitive psychologists of not explaining *where* these cognitive processes take place in the brain, because that would mean we are confusing the biological level with the information processing level. And neither neuroscientists nor cognitive psychologists should be accused of failing to provide an answer to the questions of *why* we perceive the world in a certain way, or what the overarching goals and functions of cognitive processes are. That again, would be a different level of analysis; namely, the rational level.

Just like it is important for understanding human minds to not confuse these three levels, it is important for understanding artificial minds to keep these levels apart. For AI, a focus on the physical implementation of a system, the biological level, may involve considerations related to the actual hardware and the software of the system. It may include questions about the Central Processing Unit (CPU), the choice of programming languages, the various hardware components, and the kind of data storage systems. The fact that these answers will not say much about the algorithms being used or the mathematics of the procedures being carried out is irrelevant. Questions related to the practical realization of the system simply do not need to answer questions about how the system accomplishes its computational goals. Instead, those are reserved for a different level of analysis, the one that focuses on what specific algorithms, techniques, and methodologies are used to achieve the system's goals. And neither the hardware or software level, nor the algorithms' level define what the system does and why it does it, or the purpose and objectives of the system. Again, those queries belong to a different level of analysis.

Now, what is true for distinguishing different levels of analysis in human minds, and in the analysis of artificial minds, is even more true for comparing different levels between human and artificial minds. Let's return to the example of a football game, but now consider a human football player (psychology) – you pick your favourite one – and a robot (AI). Football players may kick the ball across the field with their feet, whereas a robot may roll the ball forward with their shovel. One has legs, the other a shovel and wheels. One has a face, the other may not. The two – the psychological and the AI system – may look very different. However, regardless of the very different physical systems, the step-by-step procedures they use to achieve the goal (the football goal in the current example), the algorithms the human and robot apply may still be very much the same. Both may compute the fastest way of scoring avoiding the players of the opponent team. Thus, at the information-processing level, human and robot may be identical whereas at the biological level they may seem very different. The argument that artificial intelligence cannot reach humanlike performance because artificial intelligence does not have a human brain is thus a problematic one.

Conversely, a robot and a human may look very much alike, but the way they process information may be very different. A robot may look extremely humanlike realistic, yet the way it reaches its goal – a football related goal or not – may be very different. On the rational level, the level of the physical system, the robot may look very much the same as the human player but at the information processing level it may function very differently. Because of our anthropomorphizing tendencies, it is tempting to think that if it looks like a human, it operates like a human. Perhaps this is the reason that robots often look like humans, with arms (often two), legs (often two), and a face (often one). There is nothing at the rational or information processing level that dictates the physical system, the biological level. On the contrary. But apparently, we would like to attribute more human information processing level characteristics to a machine that looks like a human solving humanlike problems. To quote the 18th century French robot maker Jacques de Vaucanson: "If it looks like a duck, swims like a duck, and quacks like a duck, then it probably is a duck."[14] Because of the different levels of analyses discussed here, the very logic of the statement is wrong. The rational and biological levels being identical does not mean that the information-processing level is identical too.

There is one final reason to distinguish between these different levels of analyses, one that is less philosophical in nature. Discussions on artificial intelligence[15], how AI may take over our jobs, how realistic a robot looks or how a chatbot responds like a human are often driven by questions regarding the biological and rational levels. The system looks the same (or not) or solves the problem the same way (or not). AI is seen as a threat because it takes over our jobs, that is, it deals with the very nature of the problem more efficiently. A system that generates language may replace journalists or lawyers, a robot that is able to grab a product may take over the jobs of workers in logistics or maintenance. These are of course real concerns. But part of the concern should also focus on a different level, the information processing level. After all, by understanding the mechanisms of how that natural language tool or robot reaches their goals, the perception of the functionality and dangers of these systems may actually be impacted. In other words, understanding artificial minds ought to be important for understanding artificial intelligence. In the next chapters I will address these different levels. I will be starting out with the rational level: what makes artificial intelligence intelligent?

# 2

## HOW INTELLIGENT ARE HUMAN AND ARTIFICIAL MINDS?

A book about the psychology of artificial intelligence must of course discuss intelligence. Essentially, intelligence is the concept that forms the very heart of artificial intelligence, and is the most obvious common denominator between psychology and artificial intelligence. The central question in this chapter is how minds are intelligent regardless of whether they are human or artificial. After all, only when we have established what we mean by intelligence, we can address the question of what mechanisms human and artificial minds use to be viewed as intelligent.[1]

### HOW INTELLIGENT ARE HUMAN MINDS?

Let's start out with the etymology of "intelligence". The word comes from the Latin verb *intelligere*, to comprehend or perceive. By that definition, if you understand something, you are intelligent. The big question then is what constitutes that *something*. And this is the very issue that has kept researchers debating. If we can write poetry, are we intelligent? If we understand mathematics, are we intelligent? If we understand human relations, does that make us intelligent?

The confusion about the very notion of what intelligence is, is not new. It has a rich history of well over 2,500 years. In ancient Greece

DOI: 10.4324/9781003491095-2

intelligence was described by Plato as the immortal, the rational part of the human soul, in which truth and logic were apparent. True intelligence involved the ability to grasp the true nature of reality. This highest kind of knowledge, far superior to opinions or beliefs about the physical world, can be developed through education, Plato argued. This highest kind of knowledge concerns perfect, unchanging ideals of which objects in the physical world are only imperfect copies. Take for example a circle that is drawn. Any drawn circle is an imperfect representation of the perfect concept of a circle. And therefore, reaching true intelligence would be hard, very hard.

Around the same time Plato described his ideas, Aristotle described intelligence as that part of the soul that knows and understands, that reasons. However, whereas Plato argued that intelligence and knowledge are primarily innate qualities of the soul that can be reached through education, Aristotle emphasized the acquisition of knowledge through experience and education. For Aristotle, the mind starts out as a blank slate (a *tabula rasa*) and gains knowledge through sensory experiences. That is, we come to know the world through observation and experience, and intelligence is built upon the systematic collection and analysis of empirical data whereby sensory experiences provide the raw data for the intellect to process. Intelligence then is a dynamic and multifaceted capacity that developed through sensory experience, rational analysis, and the cultivation of both theoretical and practical wisdom. Theoretical wisdom combined scientific knowledge and philosophical understanding in the pursuit of truth and understanding of fundamental principles. This form of wisdom Aristotle considered the highest form of knowledge, aiming at knowing for its own sake. Practical wisdom, on the other hand, involved the ability to make good decisions in everyday life. This form of intelligence was concerned with ethical behaviour. Both education and experience, involving observation, logical analysis, and ethical training, developed theoretical and practical wisdom.

This chapter is not about the philosophy of Plato and Aristotle on intelligence. It is not to provide an extensive history of the concept of intelligence that was introduced well over two thousand years ago.

But what the description of their ideas shows is how murky the very definition of intelligence is, then but also now. Plato and Aristotle addressed questions that still dominate discussions on the concept of intelligence today. Questions such as whether we are born intelligent or become intelligent through our experiences. Whether intelligence is innate to our soul as Plato, or whether we are born with a tabula rasa, and do we become intelligent through sensory experiences and learning, as Aristotle argued? When defining intelligence, should we focus on Aristotle's theoretical intelligence or practical intelligence? And to what extent is intelligence dynamic and multifaceted?

We could try to define intelligence by how we use knowledge when we think. We could focus on Plato's true nature of reality or on Aristotle's theoretical and practical wisdom. Or we could circumvent the question on the nature of knowledge by a mechanistic approach. We then not so much ask ourselves the question of what intelligence is, but of how we can measure intelligence. Fast forward to the 19th century. The half-cousin of Charles Darwin, Francis Galton, operationalized the concept of intelligence by developing an intelligence test. Galton measured the intellectual ability of a participant through a battery of tests that measured visual acuity, grip strength, but also reaction time to sounds. Galton argued that the faster somebody responded to a sound, the more intelligent they had to be. Intelligence to him was not so much the amount of what we know, as it was the speed with which we recognize a stimulus. Intelligence to him was not so much about better reasoning, as it was about faster reasoning. No wonder that Galton is considered the founder of psychometrics, the field in psychology that investigates measuring, testing and assessing psychological phenomena. It turned out that Galton's measurements of intelligence were not very successful[2]. Technological and methodological limitations were the problem, as well as the fact that Galton primarily focused on physical and sensory measurements instead of the cognitive processes that later tests focused on.

Meanwhile, Galton's half-cousin Charles Darwin considered intellectual powers to consist of problem-solving, reasoning, and the capacity for abstract thought, which had unsurprisingly evolved over time. According to Darwin, the development of these cognitive abilities might have been influenced by the need for practical skills, such as toolmaking and language, which were important for survival and social cooperation. For Darwin, all animals were intelligent, but humans were simply more intelligent because of their adaptive processes.

Even though Francis Galton should perhaps have received the credit for developing the first IQ test[3], it was Alfred Binet who commonly receives these honours. In 1905 Binet together with Théodore Simon developed the Binet-Simon test that measured the intelligence of a student. Students were asked a series of questions, including very simple tasks such as distinguishing day from night, left from right, naming four different colours, but also reciting the months of a year, naming sixty words in three minutes, and giving the definition of abstract terms. Questions were pitched at the age level of the child. Binet and Simon were obviously aware of the fact that a 13-year-old knows things that cannot be expected from a 3-year-old. Their IQ test took this into account with questions being tailored towards a student's age. The performance on the various tasks yielded an estimated mental age, and this mental age was then divided by the actual age of the child. Thirteen-year-olds who did not master the tasks tailored at 10-year olds were simply considered less intelligent than 10-year-olds who mastered all tasks posed to them.

Apparently the Binet-Simon test was successful in measuring intelligence. After all, it is still used in the United States in a revised version, in the Stanford-Binet test. Lewis Terman, a psychologist at Stanford University, applied the Binet-Simon Intelligence Scale to the United States with his 1925 "The Measurement of Intelligence: An Explanation of and a Complete Guide for the Use of the Stanford Revision and Extension of the Binet-Simon Intelligence Scale." The Stanford-Binet test includes questions such as[4]

> If Tuesday is the third day of the month, what day of the month is the upcoming Sunday?

*Which identical five-letter word, when placed in front of the following words, forms a new word? EGO, STAR, IMPOSE, HERO.*

*This year, 16 out of 800 employees who worked for a corporation received awards for their performance, which is _____ percentage of the employees?*

For adults, David Wechsler in 1955 developed what is now the most widely used individual intelligence test for adults[5]. The current version of the Wechsler Adult Intelligence scale (WAIS) consists of six verbal and five performance subtests, ranging from comprehension and vocabulary tests to picture arrangements and object assembly. Both the Stanford-Binet and the WAIS tests are widely used for assessing 'intelligence', but the former covers a wider age range, from early childhood to adulthood, whereas the latter is specifically designed for adults.

British mathematical psychologist Charles Spearman followed Francis Galton's tradition and developed a statistical technique the relationships among test scores. This technique, called a factor analysis, identified the common dominators in a large set of data. For instance, imagine that we develop 100 different questions that a large number of people answer. We can now look at the similarities across the answers to the questions and identify which questions are consistently answered in a similar way. Apparently, these questions tap into a common aspect of the phenomenon all questions aim to address.

Let's make this a bit more concrete. Imagine a large set of questions and their test scores from a large number of participants. Factor analysis helps to find underlying factors by identifying common patterns in the data. It groups together those variables that tend to move together, presumably because they are influenced by the same underlying factor. The idea here is that someone who is high (or low) on intelligence should perform similarly across a whole range of these tests.

When Spearman studied mental ability and applied his factor analysis in 1904, he found evidence for a single factor in the analysis, which he called g, some kind of general intelligence. But in addition to this general intelligence, he found evidence for specific abilities unique to each individual test. He called this factor *s*, for specific intelligence. And thereby Spearman laid the foundation for different kinds of intelligence.

Raymond Cattell came to a compromise on rejecting the notion of Spearman's general intelligence and proposed seven independent mental abilities. Cattell pointed out that perhaps we should not speak of one intelligence, but of two kinds. A fluid intelligence that taps into the ability of solving problems, reasoning and remembering, on the one hand, and a crystallized intelligence that consists of the knowledge and ability acquired as a result of experience in your environment, including the cultural environment and schooling. It (again) suggests that we are not born with a specific level of intelligence, albeit an aspect may be hereditary. Instead, environmental factors also play a role. What can already be found in Aristotle's discussion of intelligence is what was stated by Cattell most explicitly. Intelligence was multifaceted, partly determined by nature partly by nurture.

Now what if a person is able to recite Shakespeare or is outstanding in playing the violin, but is unable to do well in math? Imagine that this person excels at the vocabulary part of an IQ test but flunks every math part of that task. According to a general intelligence point of view, the person cannot be considered intelligent. Or imagine that somebody who excels at playing chess but has difficulty reasoning through arguments made in a text? It would be odd to call the one person intelligent and the other one not. In the 1980s Howard Gardner argued that the idea needs to be rejected that intelligence can be captured through the analysis of test performance. Rather than seeking a general intelligence factor, we need to understand human behaviour as a range of unique talents and abilities. Gardner proposed eight different intelligences. In addition to the logical-mathematical intelligence, displayed in scientists and problem solvers, and linguistic intelligence shown in writers or poets, Gardner distinguished other types that extended beyond vocabulary and math (and therefore extended beyond what had been traditionally considered intelligent). For instance, he distinguished musical intelligence shown in skilled musicians, bodily-kinaesthetic intelligence displayed in athletes, interpersonal and intrapersonal intelligence for those who have excellent insights in other people's emotions or one's own emotions, and naturalistic intelligence, demonstrating insight in other species often shown in biologists and environmentalists.

Whether Gardner distinguished between different intelligences or rather between different talents is a topic of debate in psychology, but there currently is no longer a debate on the idea that intelligence is multidimensional and should not be seen as one general ability of reasoning and problem solving. Psychologists may agree it is not one intelligence, but whether it is eight intelligences or less is not clear. Most recently, Robert Sternberg argued for three dimensions. An analytical intelligence involving basic analytical skills, which can be compared to school intelligence, one's performance on school tests. A second kind of intelligence focuses on creative intelligence, the ability of dealing with novel tasks. Passing your school exams does not necessarily mean that you can apply the knowledge and skills to novel tasks. Finally, practical intelligence taps into how well we are able to solve problems posed by our cultural surroundings, for instance, knowing whether a parking space is large enough for your car. Street smart that no school knowledge you generally get prepares for in textbooks.

But in case you might think that with eight intelligences or three parts of one intelligence, we are there yet, you may want to reconsider. Remember Plato considered the rational part as the highest of the three parts of the soul and the emotions the second part of the soul, supporting the rational part. In none of the definitions of intelligence so far, our ability to deal with social relations is measured. And if there is one aspect of animal behaviour – at least that of human behaviour – that makes us survive, it is the social aspect. How we manage our emotions, how we use our emotions to manage our thoughts and actions, and how we understand the emotions of others, might be considered yet another intelligence, emotional intelligence. Indeed, the very definition of intelligence is murky.

As we saw in Francis Galton's work, we could argue that it is not only whether one can solve a particular problem, but also how *fast* that problem gets solved. This makes sense. If we compare those who perform high and low on intelligence tests, the brains of the "intelligent" people work faster than the brains of "less intelligent" people. And there is evidence that brain size and scores on intelligence tests are related.[6] That creates opportunities to measure intelligence objectively. When intelligence is associated with the speed of mental processing, and brain size matters, we then might be able to measure intelligence based on brain size. But drawing such conclusions is dicey to say the least. The relation that has been found between speed and brain size was quite small, about 10%.[7] And we also know that different kinds of brain region are related to different sizes of brain regions, making the relation between speed and size problematic. And finally, general intelligence seems to be related to increased cortex, but one could ask the question whether increased cortex *causes* increased intelligence or is simply correlated. Correlation is not causation, as any psychology student learned. Perhaps the best way to explain the difference is by using the following anecdote. At the end of a song in a U2 concert, the audience went quiet. Singer Bono then started clapping his hands rhythmically. Clap. . . clap. . . clap. . . He then picked up the microphone and explained that with every clap somebody in Africa died. Clap. . . Clap. . . Clap. . . A person at the front row then desperately yelled at him: "Please. . .! Please. . .! Stop clapping!!!" Correlation being misinterpreted as causation.

You might be happy to know that it does not take much for humans to become more intelligent. In just a few generations we will have become more intelligent. Without any additional education. Or rather, our entire population has become more intelligent over time. The so-called Flynn effect shows that every generation becomes more intelligent than its grandparents. Basically, if we scored individuals a century ago against modern norms, they would have an average IQ of 70. If we scored ourselves against the norms used a century ago, we would have an average IQ of 130[8]. There is a variety of explanations for this effect of becoming more intelligent, ranging from better health and nutrition, access to information, and education. In any case, it once again shows that intelligence is what intelligence tests measure. This circular reasoning is thought-provoking as it brings us back to the murky definition of intelligence.

## HOW INTELLIGENT ARE (NON-HUMAN) ANIMAL MINDS?

Before we move from the murky concept of human intelligence to artificial intelligence, let's step up the murkiness of intelligence a notch. After all, when we think of intelligence we generally think of human intelligence. The intelligence of the human species is superior to that of other species, so we have assumed for decades. The emphasis we have placed on intelligence, with regards to other humans and particularly with regards to other non-human animals, demonstrates how narrow-minded human minds tend to be.

First, there are plenty of examples from the animal cognition literature that show that animals are considerably smarter than we thought. Bumble bees can be taught how to play golf, or rather, how to move a little ball in a little hole in the ground for some sugary treat. Other bumble bees observing the golf moves then choose the balls closest to the holes on the ground. Kind of intelligent, if you ask me! Long-tailed macaques in Indonesia steal objects from tourists and return them in exchange for food. Albeit criminal, that is smart for a macaque! What is more, adult macaques have mastered the laws of economics. They learned to prefer stealing electronic devices, pairs of glasses, and other valuable items over objects that were less valuable for humans such as empty camera bags and hairpins in anticipation of more preferred food rewards. Criminal intelligence and economic intelligence at the same time.

Or let's take human and non-human animal intelligence a step further. Let's assume that we define intelligence by the successful completion of the following task. You sit in front of a computer screen and numbers are quickly flashed on the screen. You are then asked to tap the numbers in the right order and the right places where they appeared. You may see the number 3 in one corner, the number 6 in another, the number 7 in the middle, and you are asked to tap in the right place on the screen in the right order. Most participants are slow on this task and can reach about 5 or 6 steps, about five numbers in the right places in the right sequence. Now if we take another primate, the chimp, to perform this task, they can do this much faster than humans. And they make fewer errors, and can reach up to 8 steps. Chimps apparently can instantly form a mental snapshot of the screen. That skill would allow them to remember the locations of food or creating a mental map of a dangerous situation[9]. Chimp intelligence beats human intelligence (at least when it comes to these specific short-term memory tasks).

These are examples of cognitive tasks that humans can at least be a strong competitor with other animals. We may perform on par with other animals. We may be beaten sometimes, but on most cognitive tasks we do well, you may argue. But these examples are all based on a human centred view of intelligence. Comparing what we know we can do to what a non-human animal may (or may not) be able to do. But what if we identified intelligence differently, according to non-human standards. If we defined intelligence as the ability to comprehend something, we may for instance also argue that intelligence is determined on comprehending smell. We could define intelligence as the ability to detect objects through smell successfully. Imagine an intelligent test consisting of tasks for detecting drugs, explosives, and even diseases like cancer or COVID-19. If passing this test makes one intelligent, humans would have a very low IQ. Dogs, one the other hand, having an extraordinary sense of smell, would pass the test with flying colours. Their IQ score would be through the roof. No wonder, their smell is estimated to be 10,000 to 100,000 times more sensitive than humans.

But we can also define intelligence by the ability of visually comprehending objects. Humans would again be considered a rather unintelligent species. Their visual intelligence is certainly not in any way close to the visual intelligence of an eagle. Eagles with their incredibly sharp vision, can see prey from miles away. Their vision is about four to eight times better than that of humans. And where humans would fail this visual intelligence test, the Mantis Shrimp would pass the test as they are capable of even detecting polarized light and seeing an extensive range of colours, including ultraviolet. Humans cannot.

I can go on. When it comes to auditory intelligence, bats use their echolocation to navigate and hunt in complete darkness to determine the location, size, and shape of objects. And if you argue that using echolocation on an auditory intelligence test constitutes cheating, elephants can hear low-frequency sounds allowing them to communicate over long distances of around 6 miles and detect approaching storms. Humans cannot, allowing the conclusion that bats and elephants (and shrimp, eagles, chimps and pigeons) are far more intelligent.

Moving away from olfactory, visual and auditory intelligence, we may even want to define intelligence as the ability to navigate. Arctic Terns migrate from the Arctic to the Antarctic and back each year, covering over 50,000 miles. These birds' navigational abilities rely on the Earth's magnetic field, celestial cues. Their navigation skills are simply extraordinary. Even if we defined intelligence as navigational intelligence Arctic Terns would totally outperform humans.

My point is this. We often tend to think that humans are so much more intelligent than other animals. Now there are two options. We have to conclude that humans do have superior intelligence, but what animals demonstrate does not constitute intelligence. That is a problematic claim because over the last decades psychology has defined the concept of intelligence as being multifaceted or even considered different intelligences, so why would visual, auditory, olfactory, and navigational intelligence not fit that definition? The second option is that we have to conclude that humans are not more intelligent than other animals, for animals beat humans on different intelligences. Douglas Adams makes this point far more eloquently.

> For instance, on the planet Earth, man had always assumed that he was more intelligent than dolphins because he had

achieved so much – the wheel, New York, wars and so on – whilst all the dolphins had ever done was muck about in the water having a good time. But conversely, the dolphins had always believed that they were far more intelligent than man – for precisely the same reasons."[10]

Human intelligence has already been hard to define, but when we consider intelligence in non-human animal cognition, it shows how self-centric humans have been in defining intelligence. Over time, psychology research has shown that human intelligence is multifaceted, but that research has ignored the fact that there are many types of other (perhaps non-human) intelligences that could be distinguished. And that conclusion is of critical importance when considering *artificial intelligence*.

## HOW INTELLIGENT ARE ARTIFICIAL MINDS?

*"Will artificial intelligence ever match human intelligence?"*
*"Artificial intelligence has now reached human intelligence."*
*"Artificial intelligence can ultimately surpass human intelligence!"*

Whenever these media headlines highlight the intelligence of AI, the question that should really be asked is what (kind of) human intelligence is meant? If we were to define intelligence as logical-mathematical intelligence, then we probably have to conclude that AI surpassed human intelligence long ago. A calculator excels in logical-mathematical intelligence. And yet calculators are generally not considered the best example of artificial intelligence. The argument that can be given for calculators not to be intelligent is that they do not sense their environment and do not learn from data or experiences. Instead, they operate on the basis of predefined formulas. They do the same thing over and over again, not understanding anything of their context. They can also not function independently but are always entirely dependent on input from its user. And they lack adaptation. They do not adapt to the data they see or experience, even if they could have sensed that data. And are therefore not intelligent. But this adds a whole range of criteria to the notion of intelligence.

If sensing and adaptation of the environment are the AI criteria that calculators do not match, then thermostats certainly qualify as a prime example of AI[11]. Thermostats of their most basic kind. Thermostats are situated within, and a part of, an environment and sense that environment and act upon it, over time, and in pursuit of their own agendas and so as to effect what it senses in the future. Thermostats exhibit spontaneous actions, adapt their behaviour through past experiences, engage in communication with their user, pursue specific goals, have control over their operations, and promptly respond to changes in the environment. But just like calculators, thermostats are hardly ever considered as a major breakthrough in AI. Despite their sensing and adaption capabilities, the problem with thermostats is that they can do only one thing.

At best thermostats can be considered an example of weak AI, also called narrow AI, because of their very limited functionality. They are designed and developed for a specific, limited task or function. Weak AI distinguishes itself from strong AI, also called 'full AI', or 'human-level AI'. These days strong AI is most commonly referred to as AGI, artificial general intelligence, the holy grail of AI accomplishments. But if we translate this back to human intelligence, it becomes immediately clear why weak and strong intelligence are misnomers. Imagine a mathematician who truly excels at mathematics, but happens to perform very poorly at emotional intelligence (intrapersonal and interpersonal), at bodily-kinaesthetic intelligence as well as musical intelligence. This mathematician is only good, albeit very, very good, at mathematics. Is that person an example of weak or narrow intelligence? And by definition of human standards *not* intelligent, because the mathematician lacks AGI? And if the conclusion is that the stellar mathematician does perform at human-level intelligence, why do we then hold this against machines that hold "only" one kind of intelligence, but lack AGI?

Similarly, one could argue that AGI is supposed to reason, use strategy, solve puzzles, and make judgments under uncertainty, represent knowledge, including common sense knowledge, plan, learn, communicate in natural language, integrate these skills in completion of any given goal. But once it achieves all those asks, do we then call the machine 'artificial general intelligent'? Or should it perhaps also have consciousness? And should it have senses? And once it has senses and consciousness and excels at all these tasks, should it also have emotional intelligence?

If we have not quite identified what general intelligence in humans entails, we cannot expect that AI can ever master AGI. In the words of computer scientist John von Neumann: "You insist that there is something that a machine can't do. If you will tell me precisely what it is that a machine cannot do, then I can always make a machine which will do just that."[12]

But even if the machine will do just that, it is unlikely that such an accomplishment will convince many of us that the machine has mastered AGI. It is likely when "it will do just that" we undoubtedly come up with a task that machine is unable to do.

The problem is this. When it comes to artificial intelligence, we are continuously moving the finish line. It is as if we are running a marathon and once we reach the metaphorical finish line, the one where we have mastered humanlike intelligence, someone will move that finish line just a bit further arguing we are not quite there yet. And once we have that new finish line in sight and are ready to celebrate our AI accomplishment of finishing the achieving-human-intelligence marathon, the finish line again is moved just a bit further. This phenomenon has been dubbed the "AI Effect"[13]. Whenever we come up with an intelligent task that computers can handle, we do not at all celebrate this as evidence that AI has now reached intelligence. Instead, we are immediately ready to discount the evidence by thinking of a task that AI cannot handle.

It is as if somebody who passes the Stanford-Binet or WAIS intelligence test with flying colours is told afterwards that they should actually not be considered intelligent for they have not yet mastered musical skills. And once they redo the intelligence test successfully also demonstrating outstanding musical skills, the laureate is told that they have not really passed the intelligence test yet because of there is an added new task to be considered intelligent: playing football at Premier League level. And another one: Reciting Shakespeare. And another: Sympathizing with others.

Let me make this important issue more concrete. For decades the accomplishment of building a computer that was able to play chess was the cutting edge of knowledge engineering. It seemed to be an impossible challenge to have computers beat humans at chess, and if a computer would be able to do so, it would be evidence of true artificial intelligence. After all, it is estimated that there are at least $10^{120}$ moves to consider. Imagine that! This astronomical number, a 1 with 120 zeros is called "the Shannon number" after Claude Shannon, co-organizer of the 1956 Dartmouth workshop that coined "artificial intelligence". The number is well beyond the number of grains of sand in the Sahara dessert. Any mind, human or artificial, able to play a game of chess successfully might be considered intelligent. Allen Newell and Herb Simon, also present both at the 1956 Dartmouth workshop and the 1956 MIT workshop that launched the cognitive revolution, predicted a year later that a computer would defeat the human chess world champion a decade later[14]. Their prediction was slightly off, only by some 30 years . . . But in 1997 IBM's *Deep Blue*, a remarkable chess computer, reached the frontiers of AI by defeating world chess champion Garry Kasparov. AI had mastered chess.

AI researchers were excited, but soon people argued that a game of chess may be complex, but still only had a finite number of possibilities and very clearly defined rules. So, beating humans at chess was impressive, but the real challenge would really lie elsewhere. The real challenge, the new finish line of the metaphorical marathon, would now be for a computer to handle games with less structured environments and more possibilities. Not a game of chess, but a computer mastering the game of Go would be truly intelligent. In many respects the game of Go is far more complex than Chess. At the start of the game, each player has 361 possible moves compared to the 20 possible moves at the start for chess. The number of possible moves is also considerably larger, estimated to be at $10^{147}$

(I will spare you reading the full number with 147 zeros). Not mastering chess, but mastering Go would constitute true artificial intelligence! Some 20 years after the success of *Deep Blue*, AI had finally achieved what for long people held to be impossible. In 2016 Google's *AlphaGo* defeated Lee Sedol, a world champion Go player. AI had mastered the final frontier of intelligence!

The AI performance was considered very impressive indeed, but people immediately argued that the real challenge for AI would be to move from a deterministic environment like the game of Go, to a real-world environment where rules are not predefined, and information is incomplete. Such a real-life example where human intelligence flourishes is driving a car. Not mastering chess, not mastering Go, but mastering driving a car would constitute true artificial intelligence! And so it happened. In 2016 the first autonomous driving vehicles became operational. Tesla's Autopilot and Waymo's self-driving cars started navigating simple driving scenarios such as highway driving. AI had now definitely reached the finish line of human intelligence!

The AI performance was considered undoubtedly impressive, but soon people argued that these systems were not *really* intelligent. Intelligent as in a human intelligence. After all, these vehicles managed to drive on highways, but they were unable to handle the complexities of urban driving that humans are so good at. A highway would be relatively easy for AI, but an environment with pedestrians and traffic signals, with cars and bicycles coming from every direction, now that would constitute intelligence! You don't have to be a fortune teller to predict what will happen next. Self-driving cars are currently operational in different parts of the world. But are they intelligent? Some would argue they are not. These cars make mistakes that humans would really not make! The fact that these self-driving cars make far fewer mistakes humans do make we conveniently tend to forget. . .

With the current developments in Generative AI, whereby AI creates stories, texts, images and videos, the human-intelligence marathon finish line is pushed further and further away. Impressive indeed, that these systems can show basic creativity, but it is not really humanlike creative for they use existing data. They are not really intelligent, for they lack consciousness.

Just as with animal intelligence, it seems as if we continuously hold artificial intelligence to different standards than human intelligence. As humans we are happy to dismiss olfactory, visual, auditory, or navigational intelligence, intelligence non-human animals excel in. Apparently because we do not master those kinds of intelligence. Most cognitive skills we *do* master make it to our definition of intelligence. When a computer beats us on those cognitive skills, we are readily willing to think of a criterion – but only one that we master ourselves! – to move the finish line of intelligence. Perhaps it is a lack of self-confidence that we humans try to hide. The moment we see that animals or machines become more intelligent according to our definition of intelligence, we readily dismiss those impressive results, and conveniently move the finish line.

## HOW ARE ARTIFICIAL MINDS ALMOST REACHING INTELLIGENCE?

How good are machines at performing intelligent tasks? Marvin Minsky, one of the key players at both the Dartmouth workshop and the MIT workshop, stated: "In general, we're least aware of what our minds do best [. . .] we're more aware of simple processes that don't work well than of complex ones that work flawlessly."[15] AI researcher Hans Moravec stated in a similar vein: "it is comparatively easy to make computers exhibit adult level performance on intelligence tests or playing checkers, and difficult or impossible to give them the skills of a one-year-old when it comes to perception and mobility."[16] The idea that we often think that cognitive tasks are difficult and demand massive computing power turns out to be wrong. Instead, sensorimotor and perceptual tasks turn out to be difficult and require vast computational resources. This paradox is dubbed the Moravec Paradox. Skills we seem to acquire automatically come natural to us. Skills that we acquired later, in terms of evolution but also in our lifetime, require cognitive effort. Think of language processing, making computations, reason through problems. For artificial minds, it is just the opposite. Evolutionarily artificial minds have acquired the tasks complex for human minds early. However, the tasks simple for human minds have not yet been acquired by artificial minds.

It is true that both Minsky and Moravec made these statements in the 1980s and the field has progressed significantly since. But overall the Moravec Paradox still holds. Whereas AI has mastered many complex problems, the simplest ones remain challenging. Depending of course how you define intelligence and whether you keep the finish line in the same position.

The question whether artificial intelligence is really intelligent is synonymous to the question whether machines can really think. And as we have seen in this chapter, just like the answer to the first question depends on how you define "intelligence", the answer to the second question depends on how you define "think". Mathematician, computer science pioneer, and cryptanalyst Alan Turing realized that simply coming up with definitions of the word "think" would not get us much further. In 1950 Turing stated[17]:

> Instead of attempting such a definition I shall replace the question by another, which is closely related to it and is expressed in relatively unambiguous words. The new form of the problem can be described in terms of a game which we call the 'imitation game'.

That imitation game involves a human, a machine and an interrogator. Imagine that you sit in front of a computer screen and can communicate with an entity on the other side, a human or a machine. You can ask intelligent questions, dumb questions, make statements, give commands, and get a response from either a human or a computer on the other side, but you don't know who is who. Turing argued that if you cannot distinguish whether your conversational partner is a computer or a human, we can conclude that the machine can think. That is, according to Turing, when a computer is indistinguishable from a human, and therefore humanlike, it can therefore think. In 1950 Turing predicted:

> I believe that in about fifty years' time it will be possible to program computers, with a storage capacity of about $10^9$, to make them play the imitation game so well that an average interrogator will not have more than 70 per cent, chance of making the right identification after five minutes of questioning.

Computers have become more and more powerful, but for a computer to pass the Turing Test turned out much harder than Turing could have predicted. After fifty years, the time he had predicted, no computer had come close passing the Turing Test. An annual competition in artificial intelligence that started in the early 1990s was akin to the Turing Test. It awarded a prize to the computer program that judges considered to be the most human-like. A human judge, for instance, a reporter, science writer, or professor, held a conversation with the computer or human by typing in questions, and the human or computer would return a written answer. The human judges then evaluated whether the machine was "intelligent", could "think", was "human-like".

In 2012 celebrating the 100th anniversary of the birthday of Alan Turing, a computer seemed to pass the Turing Test[18]. In 2014 observing the 60th anniversary of Turing's death, 33 percent of the judges were convinced that same computer was human. The program was personified as Eugene Goostman, a 13-year-old boy from Ukraine. Critics, quite ready to move the metaphorical finish line now AI seemed to have crossed it, argued that it is of course easy for a computer to pass the Turing Test when that computer is personified as a 13-year-old. Young teenagers may not have the general knowledge that adults have, so a computer playing that teenager can more easily fool judges. And typos are not too much of a problem either, because of the non-native English-speaking background of Eugene. And would it not be easy to fool a judge in only a chat session? The *real* challenge, they argued – the *actual* finish line – would be fooling a judge in actual *spoken* dialogue. I wonder, would spoken dialogue ever be evidence that computers can think? When systems do, I predict the finish line is moved up a bit further again (after all, they do not use facial expressions, gestures or show consciousness).

All accomplishments made in artificial intelligence are necessarily constrained by computing power. Now imagine a computer system with unlimited size, consuming as much energy as needed, with extremely fast processing speed well exceeding what we can imagine, that takes in unrestricted amounts of information for its computations. That computer may not exhibit artificial intelligence, but artificial *superintelligence*. AI would then have a general reasoning system that does not have the cognitive limitations humans have. Some have argued that artificial general intelligence is a very likely path to superhuman intelligence[19].

Imagine that artificial intelligence were to exceed the cognitive capabilities of humans. Imagine it would be able to solve most complex problems almost instantaneously, is able to learn and understand new concepts, languages, and systems much faster than any human or artificial mind to date. It would be able to generate novel ideas and provide creative solutions no human or artificial mind ever considered. It would perceive and understand the environment better than any human or computer was able to ever before. Imagine such hyperintelligence. Now that would be evidence that artificial intelligence is intelligent! I predict it would not be. Undoubtedly by the time AI reaches that level of intelligence we will be able to come up with another human-centred definition of artificial intelligence. Undoubtedly, we will find one aspect in the system that does not quite match our humanlike expectations. Yet. When it comes to artificial intelligence it is pretty much like what we concluded for human intelligence. Artificial intelligence is what intelligence tests measure. But only the human ones.

# 3

---

# HOW DO HUMAN AND ARTIFICIAL MINDS REASON?

No matter how we may define intelligence in human and artificial minds, one fundamental aspect of any definition of intelligence includes logic and reasoning. Whether we focus on spatial, mathematical, linguistic, musical, emotional or other aspects of intelligence, when human and artificial minds manage to draw valid conclusions from new or existing information, they are often considered intelligent. But how do such intelligent humans and artificial minds reason logically?[1]

## HOW DO HUMAN MINDS REASON?

In order to explain how human minds reason, let's start out with some mental exercise. Let me present you with a logic problem.

> Once upon a time, there was a farmer, a wolf, a goat, and a cabbage. The wolf was a non-vegetarian hungry little fella, ready to devour the goat. The goat on the other hand had a vegetarian appetite, longing for a fresh cabbage. Meanwhile, a farmer had to bring the wolf, the goat and the cabbage across a river in a rowing boat, a boat that would only hold one of the three passengers – the wolf, the goat, or the

DOI: 10.4324/9781003491095-3

cabbage. The farmer realized he had a major problem on his hands. Leaving the wolf and the goat on either bank of the river would cause mayhem, and so would leaving the goat and the cabbage on either riverbank. How would the farmer manage to bring wolf, goat and cabbage across the river?

The answer to this riddle requires some deep thinking. But the question here is what goes on in our minds when trying to solve this problem. Let's consider the various steps we likely take. First, we will have to recognize the different entities – a wolf, a goat, a cabbage, a farmer – and identify some conditions on what is, and what is not, allowed in solving the problem. We know for instance that the farmer needs to move three items, but the boat can only hold one (plus the farmer), and we know some combinations cannot be left together. So, we can define some criteria:

> Criterium 1: The farmer must be present in the boat for it to move.
> Criterium 2: The farmer can take at most one other item (either wolf, goat, or cabbage)
> Criterium 3: The wolf cannot be left alone with the goat
> Criterium 4: The goat cannot be left alone with the cabbage

With these criteria in mind, we can now think through the solution of the problem. For instance, the farmer could move the wolf, but is then left with the problem that the goat and the cabbage are left together leaving an undesirable situation. He can move the cabbage, but then the wolf and the goat are left, yielding a bloodbath. So the safest bet is to move the goat, as the wolf is strictly non-vegetarian, leaving the cabbage untouched. But once the goat is on the other side, what to do next? Bringing the wolf is a bad idea, because the wolf would eat the goat. Bringing the cabbage is a bad idea, because the goat would have the cabbage for lunch. So what to do? If like the farmer we think long and hard, we may find a solution. We could start bringing the goat to the other side. Then get the cabbage to the other side, while taking the goat back. We drop off the goat, pick up the wolf, and row the wolf to the other side, leaving the carnivore with the cabbage. And finally, pick up the goat and row back. So that the farmer, wolf, goat and cabbage live long and happily after.

These reasoning steps we have just taken may be the best way we think through the wolf-goat-cabbage problem. At least I don't really see another way. The question now is what form these reasoning steps take in the human mind? This question has kept psychologists and philosophers (as well as artificial intelligence researchers) reasoning for centuries. Most researchers agree that when we solve a problem, we likely need to generate some kind of a mental model of the problem and rationally reason through the different steps. But what then is the nature of that mental model and how is it represented in human minds?

An intuitive answer to this question is that the mental model we form is linguistic in nature. We basically think and reason in language. That is an appealing idea, because language is so innate to us. If thinking is as innate to us as language is, it seems obvious we must think in language. Without any instruction, without any school, we acquire reasoning processes and acquire language. The criteria we just defined were presented in language. And I bet that when you thought through the wolf-goat-cabbage problem yourself, you were thinking out aloud quietly murmuring "okay, but then the wolf is with the goat, so that doesn't quite work! Now what?" Thinking out aloud in language is so apparent, that psychologists often use think-aloud protocols to acquire insight in the thinking processes of participants. After all, if we want to find out how people think through a problem, we basically ask them to think aloud, thereby gaining insight into their thinking processes. Language as a language of thought.

## HOW DO HUMAN MINDS REASON WITH A LANGUAGE OF THOUGHT?

Many researchers have, however, argued that language as our communication system of thought processes cannot be the answer. First of all, too often our thoughts are non-ambiguous. We may seem to be lost and confused in our thoughts, but we are never confused whether a thought meant one thing or another. Our thoughts are unambiguous. Language is notoriously ambiguous. Take for instance the sentence "Mary saw dancing gorillas in pyjamas with binoculars." I may have a very clear unambiguous thought in my mind when expressing this sentence. One where dancing gorillas in pyjamas with binocular prints are observed by a person named Mary. So how can my mental model be distinguished from yours if one language-thought can include different thoughts? And conversely, instead of one language-thought having multiple thoughts, one thought can be expressed in multiple language-thoughts. My thought of the sentence "the dog eagerly devoured its meal" is likely similar, or even identical, to that of the sentence "the canine voraciously consumed its food."

But the problem with language being the vehicle for thought is not only its ambiguity. Think about it. Some aspects of the complexity of the language of thought may generally be considered rather vague in nature, for instance, but certainly not exclusively, in terms of what a variety of things may often refer to. Got me? What would the mental representation of that long abstract sentence be? Even though you understood that sentence, language may not have been the best expression for that thought (though I do not quite know what may).

Here is another example. If I ask you to read this sentence, who is really asking who? After all, I and you is different for me the author than it is for you the reader, but when you express the same sentence, the roles suddenly reverse. Apparently, something more unique is needed than language can express.

Indeed, if humans were only able to think in language, we would have to exclude quite a few thinkers. Babies, for instance, who do not yet have language, are very well able to think through problems. When 10–13-month-olds are shown a toy behind a box and a string attached to the toy lying on a cloth, they are quickly able to reason by analogy how to get another toy by pulling on the cloth to bring the string within reach, in order to get to the toy[2]. These infants do not have language yet to reason through the problem, but they are definitely able to reason.

Or imagine being shown a large red circle and a large green square. A smaller red circle is shown to be related to the large red circle. It is now your task to choose which object is related to the large green square. Is it a small green square? A large blue square? Or a large green triangle? Well, when reasoning by analogy, if the small red circle relates to the large red circle, then the small green square relates to the large green square (despite its different size). Sarah managed to figure this out, and Sarah does not know language as we know it. Sarah is a chimp[3].

But there are other problems with idea that the language of thought is language. A whole range of problems. If I present you with the following equation: $2x = 4$ and ask you what is more similar, $5 - x = 3$ or $10 - x = 5$, you probably have no difficulty going for the first option. While getting through the problem, you were probably not using any language along the lines of thinking "two wolves", "two red squares" or "two green objects".

Okay, another one. One more to add to the list why language-as-thought is problematic. Just close your eyes when you read the following sentence (in fact, it might be better to close your eyes after reading that sentence. . .). Imagine the shape of the letter A upside down. What does it look like? Now turn the shape 45 degrees. What does it look like now? You can now open your eyes again. If you managed to think through this task, it is most likely you managed to think through it without language.

If language is too scruffy and imprecise, and if babies who have not quite mastered language, and animals who have no human language, do show evidence of reasoning, what then would be the language of thought? We know that we need two things. One is some kind of unique representation. One where there is no confusion about who is in pyjamas with binocular prints on them watching gorillas. Secondly, we need reasoning steps for the problem at hand. Some kind of a so-called algorithm. One where a set of rules is to be followed. An algorithm that is not restricted to wolfs, goats and cabbages, but one that could also be applied when the wolf was a placeholder for something (let's say w), the goat for something else (let's call it g), and the cabbage yet for something else (perhaps c), and given the criteria outlined before (w cannot be with g and g cannot be with c). Basically, we need some kind of mathematics. The language of mathematics is non-ambiguous, is not scruffy, is fully transparent and entirely logical. But what then would a mathematical-language-of-though look like?

If the language of thought is not language itself, it likely has to be something that is at least common to language, but not dependent on the language one speaks. If you speak another language than English (or Chinese, or Spanish, or French) you do not think differently. So the language of thought we are looking for requires idea units that look like words in a language but are not. Some have argued that this language of thought can best be understood as mentalese – a mental language. Philosophers argued for such a non-linguistic language of thought. They stated that the mind operates on concepts and rules, allowing for the generation of complex thoughts and inferences. The kind involved in the wolf, goat and cabbage problem. The word "wolf", "goat", "cabbage" or "farmer" would be represented by the mentalese concept WOLF, GOAT, CABBAGE, or FARMER, and the word "move" would be represented by the mentalese event MOVE. It is very hard to use mentalese without using words, so the mentalese concepts (in capitals) are not really words but represent the meaning of words in a language. Using mentalese syntax, we can then generate mentalese sentences such as

MOVE(FARMER, GOAT)
MOVE(FARMER, WOLF)
MOVE(FARMER, CABBAGE)

Mentalese concepts and predicates are written down as a useful notational shortcut. Using logic we can create more complex mentalese sentences. For instance,

IF LEFTBANK(WOLF) AND
IF NOT LEFTBANK(CABBAGE) THEN
MOVE(FARMER, WOLF)

These propositions consist of symbols (FARMER, WOLF, GOAT, CABBAGE), relations (MOVE, LEFTBANK) and logical connectives (NOT, AND, IF-THEN). With these mentalese rules, we can now argue that we are developing a general problem solver, a set of rules that are universal in the world we have defined.

The logic of propositions, called propositional logic or propositional calculus, allows us to compute truth values from propositions. For instance, we could take the proposition IF(MONDAY, TODAY) THEN (GOWORK, MAX). That means that if today is Monday, a person named Max needs to get to work. It also means that if today is not a Monday (for instance, because it is a Tuesday) it does not mean that Max does not need to get back to work. Quite a few negations in one sentence, but it basically means that the proposition "If it is Monday, Max needs to get to work" means that if it is not Monday, Max may or may not get to work (after all, it could be either Tuesday when Max needs to go to work or Saturday when Max is off for work). Only when it is Monday, Max needs to go to work. Propositional logic is powerful. It helps us to reason through mathematical problems and humans have the mind to do.

Indeed, rules like these can help us through the day. Whether it is moving wolfs, goats and cabbages across the river, or deciding on the next chess move, or deciding whether I need to go to work, in essence propositional logic is a general problem solver. If I am thirsty, I grab a glass of water. If I wake up, I make myself a coffee. If I am tired, I go to bed OR I make myself a coffee.

Glad that we have sorted out some human reasoning. Reasoning of human minds explained in only a few pages. Quite an accomplishment! Of course, things turn out to be far more complex, as the language of thought issue has kept philosophers and psychologists busy for centuries. The mental models may nicely provide an internal representation of an external reality that plays a major role in cognition, particularly in reasoning and decision-making. Propositions as a representation of the language of thought is indeed appealing, as it solves issues that the language-thought had, and it looks language enough to be intuitive[4]. The question is whether these propositions are more than a simplified representation? Are they just a shorthand notation, just as a shopping list is a shorthand notation to remind us of what we need to do at the grocery store? Or are they psychologically real?

Discourse psychology, the field of psychology that investigates how humans understand multi-sentence texts and dialog, have found evidence that humans do not remember sentences verbatim, but extract the gist of these sentences. For instance, whether a sentence was stated in an active ("the farmer moved the goat") or a passive form ("the goat was moved by the farmer") tends to be easily forgotten, but the fact that there was a moving event by a farmer that involved a goat does not. And this abstraction of the actual language is what propositions are all about. It is as if we extract meaningful idea units from the information we hear or see, idea units of the kind propositions represent.

Let's sum up. So far we have dismissed *language* as the language-of-thought and replaced it by *propositions* as the language-of-thought. These propositions may have their advantages, but they cannot be the entire story. Reasoning very much relies on implicit and contextual information. Take for instance the following story: Mary heard the ice cream man coming. She remembered her pocket money. She rushed into the house[5]. We could formulate mentalese rules such as HEAR(MARY, ICECREAM MAN) and REMEMBER(MARY, MONEY) but there is a whole bunch of idea units that go on in our minds when we read this three-sentence story. Apparently there is a girl, named Mary, who hears an ice cream man coming, a guy who probably drives an ice cream van. Mary knows that when an ice cream man comes, he sells ice cream. Contemplations such as Mary probably wanted an ice cream pop up. And that Mary knew that an ice cream costs money. And that Mary knew that she did not have (enough) money with her and needed (additional) money. And that

Mary remembered her pocket money that may be used to buy ice cream. If we describe thinking in a mathematical matter, as propositions try to do, we do not only need the propositions that are stated in the problem and the criteria that help us to solve the problem. We also need to identify all propositions in the world (our mental world and out physical world) that are going into the reasoning process. And creating a database of all the thoughts we think when solving a problem or understanding a story is difficult.

## HOW DO ARTIFICIAL MINDS REASON?

The philosophical and psychological answer as to how we reason has – albeit perhaps inadvertently – strongly been influenced by the question of how computers reason. Propositional logic dominated cognitive psychology in the latter half of the 20th century as the solution as to how human minds reason. This was exactly around the time that computers became commonplace. When reading about the language of thought and the propositional logic of IF-THEN rules, you may have wondered: that logic almost looks like computer code! Indeed, the rules for the wolf, goat and cabbage problem can easily be translated into computer code. While psychologists thought about mental representations with computational modelling, artificial intelligence researchers thought about algorithmic processes with cognitive models in mind.

How then would an artificial mind solve the wolf-goat-cabbage problem? It would follow a systematic approach, one it often uses for solving a state-space search problem[6]. It would first define the State Representation, representing each state by their respective positions. It would identify for each item, F, W, G, C (abbreviations for farmer, wolf, goat and cabbage) an initial state and a goal state. The initial state for these four items would be one side of the river first, let's say the left side [L, L, L, L] and a goal state for all four items, let's say the right side [R, R, R, R]. Next, transition rules need to be defined, such that the wolf and the goat cannot be left alone together without the farmer and the goat, and the cabbage cannot be left alone together without the farmer. After having defined the valid states, for instance that no invalid pair (wolf and goat, goat and cabbage) should be left alone a Search Algorithm can start exploring all possible states. With each of the four items (F, W, G, C) being in one of two positions (L, R), we ultimately end up with:

> Farmer takes the goat across the river: [L, L, R, L]
> Farmer returns alone: [R, L, R, L]
> Farmer takes the wolf across: [R, R, R, L]
> Farmer returns with the goat: [R, R, L, L]
> Farmer takes the cabbage across: [L, R, L, R]
> Farmer returns alone: [R, R, L, R]
> Farmer takes the goat across: [R, R, R, R]

Solving complex problems has now been reduced to applying logic-based techniques to manipulate symbols to systematically explore the solution space. This way artificial minds will always end up with a valid true solution. And with all the rules of the system being explicit, artificial minds (and human minds alike) always have full control over what happens in the system.

Just as with propositions in human thinking, for simple problems such as the wolf-goat-cabbage problem defining the knowledge base and the logical rules are manageable. Perhaps for an expert system such as the wolf-goat-cabbage system, such a rule system is convenient. For other expert systems that are less fictional, such as real-world medication systems this is no different. It is possible to state that if medication A is taken, medication B should not be taken, or that medication B should only be taken if medication A is taken, but not when medication C is taken.

But the *real* real-world problems even need more. Imagine representing common knowledge. If all the knowledge is listed that is needed to solve actual problems in the world, creating the knowledge base with concepts and rules will become a daunting task. And yet, encouraged by the promise and enthusiasm, several attempts have been made to represent the knowledge of the world in propositional logic.

Let me illustrate some of these computational attempts by using Shakespeare's *Romeo and Juliet*. Let me help you brush up on your Shakespearean knowledge: Our main actor Romeo spent the night with Juliet, consummating their marriage. But there is a problem. Juliet's father agrees to marry his daughter to a count and threatens disowning Juliet if she refuses. Seeking help from a friar, Juliet is given a potion inducing a 24-hour deathlike coma. She can fake her own death and does not have to marry the count. Romeo will then be informed of the plan so that he can rejoin Juliet when she wakes up. On the eve of the wedding between Juliet and the count, Juliet takes the potion. She is presumed to be dead and put to rest in the family crypt. Everything seemed to be going well, except that the message of the plan of faking Juliet's death fails to reach Romeo. Instead, Romeo learns from a servant that Juliet passed away. Romeo is devasted. He purchases a poison, and believing the love of his life is gone, drinks the poison. A while later Juliet awakens. Surprised she discovers Romeo's death. And seeing her lover been gone, she stabs herself with Romeo's dagger. Romeo and Juliet are united again, albeit in death.

Understanding this story – the actual play is considerably more pleasant to read and is much better written – requires many propositions and relations between propositions. For one thing, each concept needs to be identified. This seems easy in human minds. When it comes to the psychological concept of propositions, much can conveniently be assumed: We know what a wolf, goat and cabbage are; we know that an ice cream van is driven by an ice cream vendor and that when ice cream is sold, you need money; we know that Romeo is not a wolf, goat or ice cream man, or an ice cream van. For a human mind all this is pretty obvious. But for artificial minds this is a very different story. Each and every concept, each and every move, all aspects of the context need to be carefully written out for a language of artificial thought.

## HOW DO ARTIFICIAL MINDS REASON WITH A LANGUAGE OF ARTIFICIAL THOUGHT?

George Miller is considered one of the founders of cognitive psychology and cognitive science. He was one of the attendees of the MIT workshop in 1956 the one that initiated the cognitive revolution, two months after the Dartmouth workshop that coined artificial intelligence. In the late 1960s Miller launched the idea to build a computational lexical database that would be consistent with theories of human semantic memory. An artificial mind that matched the human mind. Two things are noteworthy here. One is that it was a cognitive psychologist who launched the idea of a computational database of human knowledge. Second, that the idea was launched in the 1960s. Miller realized that understanding human minds might benefit from developing artificial minds (and vice versa). A psychology of artificial intelligence. Whereas the propositional networks described earlier were a theoretical construct, Miller developed an actual application that could be used for natural language processing. One where the capitalized concepts in propositions were no place holders for mentalese, but ones where they were defined and where relations with other words were given.

It took a while, but in 1985 the first version of that database, called WordNet, became available. WordNet has now become a massive lexical database of semantic relations between words. Semantic relations that included synonyms, words with a similar meaning. Hyponyms and hypernyms, words that are a subset or a superset of other words, such as Golden Retriever being a subset of dog, and dog being a superset of Golden Retriever. And meronyms where a word concept is part of another word concept, such as toe being part of a foot. WordNet consists of 155,327 words that are linked this way. A massive enterprise! If one person were to take on this task and write the code for one word every hour of every day, it would take 17 years to complete WordNet. But once this task is accomplished, one has a major resource for computational linguistics and artificial intelligence. WordNet became so popular that it has now been used across the world in many dozens of languages, from Arabic to Chinese, from Malay to Telugu[7].

Back to the Shakespearean play. How would WordNet represent the concepts in *Romeo and Juliet*? The answer to that question would require at least a chapter, and likely more than one, given the many concepts in the play. And it would not be the most exciting reading. I will therefore only focus on the WordNet representation of one concept, that of the main character Romeo.

- **Romeo** (an ardent male lover)

  *direct hypernym* / **inherited hypernym** / *sister term*

- S: (n) lover (a person who loves someone or is loved by someone)
- S: (n) person, individual, someone, somebody, mortal, soul (a human being) *"there was too much for one person to do"*
- S: (n) organism, being (a living thing that has (or can develop) the ability to act or function independently)
- S: (n) entity (that which is perceived or known or inferred to have its own distinct existence (living or non-living))
- S: (n) causal agent, cause, causal agency (any entity that produces an effect or is responsible for events or results)
- S: (n) physical entity (an entity that has physical existence)
- S: (n) entity (that which is perceived or known or inferred to have its own distinct existence (living or non-living))

With the success of WordNet, other computational linguistic tools emerged that built on WordNet.

Basically what WordNet did is develop a system of databases that would allow for a propositional representation of the world around us. It answered the question of a mental model computationally. It developed an artificial mind that was humanlike. So far, so good. But knowing the meaning of a single concept (or single proposition) does not get us far. It does not really allow for reasoning through the story of *Romeo and Juliet*. For instance, human minds know that if a person were dead, they would not have to marry anyone. Human minds know that if someone drinks a fatal dose of poison, they immediately die. That if one believes that the love of one's life has just died, then the person is likely to feel overwhelming sadness and hopelessness. That if someone dies, they stay dead. So how can we feed all these pieces of information to artificial minds? That computational exercise would be even more overwhelming.

Around the time George Miller started WordNet to map out the meaning of words, Douglas Lenat began an even more ambitious project. It already is an incredible daunting task to develop a taxonomy of concepts, but it seems to be even more daunting to code the countless pieces of knowledge that make up human common sense. It did not stop Lenat to build a database of statements and an inference engine that allowed to reason though these statements. The project was dubbed Cyc.[8] All the pieces of knowledge were at least initially entered manually by Cyc staff. A few years ago, Cyc's ontology consisted of 24.5 million terms that took over 1,000 person-years of effort to construct. Following the Romeo and Juliet example, rules would for instance consist of the following:

— if a person were dead, they would not have to marry anyone.
— if someone drinks an instantly fatal dose of poison, they immediately die.
— if a trusted friend of yours tells you something, and you don't have a better reason not to believe it, then you are very likely to believe what they say.
— if one believes that the love of his/her life has just died, then he/she is likely to feel overwhelming sadness and hopelessness.
— if someone dies, they stay dead.
— an object at rest will stay at rest until moved by some person or some force acting on that object.
— while anyone is unconscious or dead, they are an object at rest.

Now if we ask the question "When she takes the feign-death potion, does Juliet believe Romeo will believe she is alive during the time she is in suspension?" Cyc will answer:

Yes. If, at time T1, an agent's model of a subject's beliefs at time T2 includes a proposition, then the agent believes at T1 that the subject believes the proposition at T2. At the time of Juliet's taking of the of the feign-death potion, Juliet has a model of Romeo's beliefs at the time of Juliet's being in suspension after taking the feign-death potion that includes the proposition that Juliet is a living thing.[9]

It is somewhat ironic that instead of language as an answer to the question how human and artificial minds think, propositions were proposed. And yet in order to pursue the propositions answer, the scientific community relied on language-related tools. It is as if the language of thought discussion yielded the thought of language. And that the question how human minds reason yielded the question how artificial minds do this.

## HOW ARE ARTIFICIAL MINDS GOOD OLD-FASHIONED?

Just like human minds can reason logically through propositions, artificial minds can. Propositional logic provides a waterproof solution to problem solving. And where the exact nature of propositions in the human mind may be somewhat evasive – researchers called it mentalese for lack of a better concept – the nature of propositions in artificial minds are very clear. Propositions in artificial intelligence are unambiguous pieces of code. Propositions are true or false, and their logic is consequently true or false. Take for instance deductive reasoning:

If it is raining, then the streets are wet.
It is raining.
Therefore, the streets are wet.

There is no ambiguity, just simple and solid logic. If it is raining, the streets are wet. If it is not raining, the street can still be wet. And if the streets are not wet, it is not raining. However, sometimes this water-proof logic leads to confusion. Let's take the following example:

> If you read this book, you wear red socks.
> You read this book.
> Therefore, you wear red socks.

You may immediately object this is a problem. You read this book, and you don't wear red socks (unless this of course happens to be the day that you are wearing your favourite red socks). So apparently propositional logic is not that waterproof. It is important to keep in mind that the propositional logic above remains valid, regardless of whether or not you chose to wear your happy red socks today. Whether the argument is sound is a very different issue.

Propositional logic has proven to be extremely powerful in psychology and artificial intelligence. Allen Newell and Herbert Simon stated about human and artificial minds that "a symbol . . . system has the necessary and sufficient means for general intelligent action"[10] In more common language: "A system that uses symbols is both required (necessary) for, and by itself enough (sufficient) to achieve, general intelligent behaviour." The philosopher Hubert Dreyfus echoed the same argument for human minds, stating "the mind can be viewed as a device operating on bits of information according to formal rules."[11]

The latter half of the 20th century showed a range of cognitive models implemented in machines. These symbolic systems, these early artificial minds, provided transparency in understanding reasoning processes, making it easier to understand how a system arrived at a conclusion. They represented complex knowledge in a formal and structured way. And they allowed for easy manipulation and reasoning. That turned out to be very useful. Because these symbolic systems were flexible, they could be adapted to different domains simply by modifying the rules and the knowledge base. The age of artificial intelligence where these symbolic systems reigned supreme was called Symbolic AI. Conclusions were based on solid logic and reasoning and allowed for transparency how conclusions were reached.

Despite the fact that Symbolic AI was heralded, over time its limitations became visible. If the world were to be simple and transparent, Symbolic AI solutions would be successful. Expert systems that mimicked the decision-making ability of a human expert in a specific domain did very well with Symbolic AI solutions. Planning and scheduling systems where tasks needed to be arranged and ordered to achieve their goals excelled in their computational task. Diagnostic systems that identified faults in complex systems reached impressive results. Automated reasoning systems that used logical inference and deduction from a set of premises drew conclusions that were simply remarkable. But all these Symbol AI systems performed on closed tasks.

After all, for Symbolic AI to function properly, it required complete and well-defined knowledge to function correctly. WordNet and Cyc are extremely useful tools, but when exceptions come up, these systems fail. What if the wolf in the wolf-goat-cabbage problem were a vegetarian? What if the farmer could in fact bring a heavy wolf but a very light cabbage across the river at the same time? What if Mary was lactose intolerant and never ate any ice creams, but realized that the ice cream man was known to be a convicted burglar? If knowledge is incomplete, the Symbolic AI system would fail. And knowledge is easily incomplete.

Even for a clear well-defined domain with clearly defined rules, such as chess, knowledge is easily incomplete. In chess $10^{120}$ moves are possible. That is, if we only take into account the valid moves. That is an incredible number! But that is chess. For a domain where the number of pieces go well beyond black and white pieces, the moves well beyond the options on a chess board, and the outcome well beyond winning or losing, the number of moves well exceed the astronomical number of $10^{120}$! And this is only under the assumption of information being precise and unambiguous. Too often, however, in the world we live in, information is uncertain or ambiguous.

But let's not be pessimists, let's be optimists! Let's assume that regardless of the amount information or its complexity we were nevertheless able to identify the massive number of symbols and rules. Imagine that we somehow put all our efforts together and managed one day to settle on a database with all the symbols and rules. We would still face a major problem. That problem is that the solution would not be scalable. With any additional piece of information, any new symbol, any new rule, it would computationally be extremely expensive to update the system. Unlike true intelligent minds, the system would not allow for real-time learning and adaptation. Despite its promise, Symbolic AI over time became more commonly and more affectionately known as Good old-fashioned AI (GOFAI). It was good, but also old-fashioned.

## HOW ARE ARTIFICIAL MINDS FUZZY EATERS?

The advantage of propositional logic is that it is clear and precise. There is no ambiguity with statements as they are either true or false, making it ideal for reasoning through problems in terms of mathematics or logic. It ensures logical consistency making it a powerful tool for ensuring valid conclusions. But in its elegant mathematical simplicity also lies its problem.

In the real world, we often deal with problems where precision and certainty are not attainable. Instead, in the real world we deal with imprecise, vague, and gradual information. Things are not always black and white. It is not always hot or cold. It may be warm, or rather hot, or too hot. It may be somewhat chilly or may be freezing. In the mid 1960s mathematician Lotfi Zadeh recognized that the world is not black and white. Zadeh proposed fuzzy logic as an extension to propositional logic[12]. Fuzzy logic would be able to deal with vague and imprecise information. Whereas there was no room for grey in propositional logic, fuzzy logic would be able to handle ambiguity and uncertainty, providing a more nuanced and realistic model for everyday situations. I will not go into the mathematical detail of fuzzy logic, but will illustrate this with some of the main characters in this chapter, the wolf, the goat and the cabbage.

In the wolf-goat-cabbage problem we assumed a very hungry wolf and a very hungry goat, who could not be left off-guard. But imagine that the wolf had just had a meal, and the goat was not particularly hungry either. With fuzzy logic we can compute degrees of the risk that the wolf would eat the goat, or the goat would eat the cabbage. For instance, the hunger level of the wolf and goat could be set at .2, but hunger levels would go up the longer the farmer left the animals alone. With low risk levels where wolf and goat were not at all hungry, the farmer may decide to leave wolf, goat or cabbage together. Only with higher risk, where hunger would reach peak levels, he should definitely not do that. Based on any value between hungry and not-hungry the farmer could therefore adjust his decisions. For example, he might take the cabbage first if the goat's temptation to eat had grown, or he might decide to transport the wolf if its hunger were to rise too quickly.

Fuzzy logic does more justice to the world we live in, and seems to offer exciting opportunities extending propositional logic. It would combine the rigor and consistency of propositional logic with the flexibility so common to us. But even though the wolf, goat, and cabbage problem might become more realistic with fuzzy logic – in so far as wolf, goat, and cabbage problems can be realistic in the first place of course – the number of conditions and the amount of variability would drastically increase. Indeed, despite the advantage of fuzzy logic dealing with more realistic problems – problems in the real-world are generally not as black and white as propositional logic would like to see them – fuzzy logic can quickly become complex especially in systems with different elements and interactions. The elegance of simplicity in propositional logic gets sacrificed by fuzzy logic. Moreover, fuzzy logic does not provide the same level of formal proof and consistency as propositional logic, with variability that is harder to quantify and prove rigorously. In addition to Symbolic AI, in addition to good old-fashioned AI, artificial intelligence also needed more sophisticated systems that would not be bogged down by a complex system of rules, yet would be able to deal with the uncertainty and imprecision of the real world.

## HOW ARE HUMAN MINDS FLAT?

This chapter has listed problems on how humans and artificial minds can reason, one after the other. Perhaps suitably for a chapter on reasoning, but problems nevertheless. In closing this chapter, I need to list yet another problem with human minds as logical machines that distinguish them from artificial minds as logical machines. Machines reason logically with propositional logic, fuzzy logic or otherwise. Consequently, they reach valid conclusions. Their reasoning process is sound. We have seen that these artificial minds are built after human minds. The problem we close this chapter with is that human minds commonly do not reason logically. Instead, we often (very often) rely on our gut. As Daniel Kahneman argued, human minds often (too often) think fast rather than slow[13]. As Gerd Gigerenzer stated, we often (too often) rely on our gut feelings when making decisions[14]. As Nick Chater provocatively claimed: our mind is flat![15] Logic too often escapes us psychologically. Let me give some examples of our flaws in reasoning, and fittingly choose examples that concern reasoning about AI.

If you tried out ChatGPT, DeepSeek, or any other Generative AI assistant, you may have judged the chatbot extremely human-like. And indeed, these applications seem to behave very much like humans. You may have concluded that all AI systems, including medical AI or industrial robots, will eventually exhibit human-level consciousness and emotions. But concluding this means that you fall in the trap that is called representativeness heuristic. You would make a judgment about the probability of an event (any AI application) being representational in character and essence of a known prototypical event (the specific AI assistant). You mistakenly generalize. Most AI systems are task-specific and are not designed to mimic human cognition. An artificial mind would hardly ever do this. Human minds do this all the time. An example of fast thinking, gut feelings, with a flat mind.

Here is another example. You read about a self-driving car that is entirely operated by AI. That car caused a major accident. An accident caused by a self-driving vehicle! You always knew. AI should never be trusted. After all, this is the evidence that AI technologies are unsafe. But as common as this reasoning may be, you just fell into the availability heuristic trap, whereby your judgment is based on the most available information of a single accident, but does not consider the broader context of the millions of miles driven safely by AI-controlled cars. Fast thinking, gut feeling, flat mind.

Or imagine you are an AI researcher asked to build a robot Wimbledon tennis player (Just hang on! If you prefer a robot for football, cricket or golf, the example works equally well). You happen to have engineered the movements of the robot arms, and are now working on the robot's artificial mind. A series of algorithms manage to compute the angle with which the ball is thrown, kicked, or swung, and the distance that it needs to travel. You continuously monitor the angle of the ball and carefully compute with high probability where it lands. Your robot with its artificial mind can start playing its first matches. But no human mind in a tennis player (or cricket, football or golf player) would make these computations. Instead, human minds use their gut feeling and are therefore not as precise. The upside is that they can make these decisions very quickly, adjust easily, and can deal with imperfect information better. They just guess where the ball is most likely to land and go for it (the evidence is that a tennis player does not have to be stellar in mathematics to still be outstanding at playing tennis).

Most of the time human minds do not at all reason logically. We just catch that ball by making estimates that are not mathematically driven. We just happen to fall in love and do not carefully assess the qualities of our catch by making a list of advantages and disadvantages (propositional logic) that we assign weights to (fuzzy logic). We make a purchase without thinking it through. Yes, we know that expensive brand name overcharges, and yes, we know that the quality of that product is not worth 10 times the price, but before we realize it, we leave the shop with our shopping bag, the virtual or paper one. Artificial minds using logic, the fuzzy or the non-fuzzy one, would never make such misjudgements. Contrary to human minds, they would not be led astray by their gut feeling. They would not make that very expensive purchase knowing all too well that it is not worth the money. They would not fall in love and choose a partner without meticulously doing the checks and balances. They would carefully and precisely reason through the conditions and come to the only valid conclusion.

When it comes to reasoning, research into human minds has influenced research into artificial minds. And research into artificial minds has influenced research into human minds. However, we just concluded that there are differences between the way human and artificial minds think. To shed light on how human and artificial minds think, we should perhaps move from the level of information-processing (central to the current chapter) to the biological level, the architecture of the human and artificial mind (central to the next chapter).

# 4

---

# HOW DO HUMAN AND ARTIFICIAL MINDS THINK?

It comes as no surprise that human minds are well equipped for thinking. After all, it is our minds that make us humans so special, so smart and so intelligent. At least that's what we ensure ourselves. Now, if the human mind is what the human brain does, it is worthwhile to better understand the apparatus that generates the human mind. The structure of the human brain might help us understand the mind and its mental processes. And it might shed light on the architecture that makes artificial minds think.[1]

## HOW DO HUMAN BRAINS THINK?

The brain, the animal brain and therefore the human brain, is part of a larger nervous system[2]. This massive and highly complex biological system sends messages back and forth between the brain and the body. Just like an air traffic control system takes information from various sources to coordinate aircrafts through airspace, the nervous system integrates information from various sources. It, for instance, takes the information coming from the sense organs and transmits this information to different parts of the nervous system. Based on the incoming sensory information, the nervous system makes decisions how to respond to these incoming signals. It decides on

DOI: 10.4324/9781003491095-4

movements, reflexes, and organ activities, just like air traffic controllers make decisions on aircraft movements. And just like air traffic controllers adjust their decisions to changes in the environment, the central nervous system makes changes based on different conditions and experiences, adjusting its responses over time.

The nervous system consists of two parts: a central nervous system that includes the brain and the spinal cord, and the peripheral nervous system that branches out from the brain and the spinal cord and consists of the nerves. Most commonly we talk about the central nervous system, with the brain playing the leading role. Central to the nervous system are nerve cells, or neurons. These neurons transmit signals across the entire nervous system. Some neurons transmit signals that we sense from the physical world around us to the brain. Not surprisingly, these are called sensory neurons. Others are equally unsurprisingly called motor neurons, as they transmit information from the brain to the muscles. In addition, there are interneurons, located in the brain and the spinal cord. These interneurons act as a middle link in the nervous system, helping to process information and relay signals between sensory and motor pathways. To get a sense of the distribution of these three types of neurons: We have about 500,000 motor neurons that control voluntary and involuntary movements by transmitting signals from the nervous system to muscles. We have twenty times more sensory neurons, some 10 million in the human body that detect stimuli from the external environment or internal organs and send information to the nervous system. But the majority of neurons in the human nervous system are interneurons. About 86 billion or more! And they are primarily located in the brain. These interneurons are responsible for the complex processing, integration, and modulation of sensory inputs and motor commands.

Interneurons are important. No wonder we have so many of them. Imagine you pick up your boiling hot cup of coffee in the morning. Your fingers touch the cup and your sensory neurons go: "Hey, this is hot! This is really, really hot!" By having interneurons, the sensory neurons can quickly communicate to the motor neurons to take action, for instance leaving the cup on the counter rather than picking it up. But the interneurons might also mitigate the process by conducting a welcome intervention in the message to the motor neurons. After all, the floor of your favourite coffee place would otherwise become a mess with your sensory neurons always telling your motor neurons to drop your cup of steaming coffee because it is hot. Your interneurons basically help to decide whether it would be wise to drop the cup and prevent injury or to hold on for your daily dose of caffeine. They modulate the information. Pretty much like the air traffic control system mentioned earlier.

The size of each of these neurons – sensory, motor, and interneurons – in the nervous system is minute, about the size of the thickness of plastic wrap or a human hair. When vastly magnified, each neuron looks somewhat like a tree with big strong roots on one end and somewhat smaller branches on the other. The root-side consists of so-called dendrites, from the Greek word δένδρον or tree. These dendrites – the network of roots – pick up chemical signals from neighbouring neurons. The cell body of the neuron picks up this signal passed on from thousands of other neurons. If the signal is strong enough, and reaches a particular threshold, it passes on electrical impulses through the small 'trunk' of the tree (called the axon) up to the 'branches' of the tree. At the end of the branches are terminal buttons (axon terminals) that reach out to other dendrites to pass on chemical signals. These chemical signals, or neurotransmitters, come in different kinds. Some are responsible for arousal and alertness, others for motivation and reward, yet others reduce anxiety.

Neurons communicate with each other by firing electrical signals down their axons, so called action potentials. This happens when the neuron receives enough input from other neurons to reach a certain threshold. The signal then travels down the axon to the end, where it activates other neurons. A typical neuron fires somewhere between 1Hz (one spike per second) to 200 Hz (200 spikes per second). If you compare that with the speed of light, a signal of a neuron may move along only at 77 yards (70 metres) per second. That is fast, but light travels some 4 million times faster! That may seem surprising because thinking appears to happen to us so fast. At the speed of light we think our thoughts. And yet the speed of light is millions of times faster than the transmissions of signals in the brain. The answer to the question why neurons seem to travel at the speed of light but are not travelling at the speed of light does not lie in the transmission process, but in the very way these signals are sent across the brain. Neurons do not transmit signals in sequence, whereby neuron A fires to neuron B, which fires to neuron C. Instead, neurons transmit information in parallel, neuron A firing to neuron B and C (and D and E and F) at the same time. One neuron may activate thousands of other neurons simultaneously. Compare it with a virus going around during the flu season. It is not the case that one person sneezes, the other person becomes sick, who might then infect another person, so that a chain reaction causes a larger group being bedridden with flu symptoms. Instead, a virus distributes with one person who carries the flu virus who infects another larger group of people, who infect another large group. And before you know it, you have a pandemic of activation, as we see every year during flu season, whereby the virus spreads exponentially. Similar to the spreading of a virus, there is a spreading of activation in the brain's network.

Neurons activate other neurons with the release of neurotransmitters. These neurotransmitters are the messengers, tiny chemicals that enable brain and body to talk to each other. It is tempting to think that one neuron or neurotransmitter holds actual information as we know it; an entire idea, a thought or concept that gets released to other neurons. That when we think of our dog or cat, that we have a neuron that is dedicated to our dog or cat that spreads information throughout the network so that all events of our dog or cat come to mind. A 'dog neuron' or 'cat neuron'. This is not at all the case. All the information a neuron carries is whether or not it fires. Basically, no single neuron carries any information other than being on or off, that we represent by a 1 or $0^3$. Instead, it is a pattern of activation across a large body of neurons that make up a thought. So a dog might be a conglomeration of neurons that fire and do not fire, say 1 0 0 1 1 1 0 1 1 1 1 1 0 0 0 0 1 1 1 1 1. A cat on the other hand a pattern of activation that is for instance 111011100000101011101. You get the idea.

Let's illustrate the notion of a network of neurons a bit more using the metaphor of dominoes. Across the world so called domino challenges, or domino rallies, are organized. Teams of people stack up dominoes – the record is currently 4.5 million of them. Stacking up is not the exciting part, bringing the network of dominoes down is the electrifying bit. Patterns of domino activation! The toppling of these networks of dominos is achieved by standing dominoes on end and arranging them in very large configurations. When the first domino is knocked over, it strikes others, which knocks down the next group, and so on, to create a chain reaction. It is not the case that one domino knocks over one domino, and moves on to the next. Instead it knocks over many. Just as dominos create a pattern of activation, neurons can activate hundreds or even thousands of neurons at the same time, creating a pattern of activation. Had each domino only knocked over one other domino, the activation would have been in sequence. But because patterns of activation appear simultaneously, in parallel, a parallel distributing process emerges across the domino network. Just like neural activation. But the similarities between domino and neural networks do not stop there. When a domino knocks over another neuron, it does so in a rather constant speed. It is not knocking over another one a bit 'more or less'. Instead, the 'action potential' is constant in an all-or-nothing fashion. For neurons, it is the same thing. Dominos fall or they don't, neurons fire, or they don't. When a domino piece falls, it takes a bit of time to put them back up, so they can be knocked over again. The same is true for neurons. They don't need to be put back up again, but they do have a recovery period after they fire, a short refractory period.

The pattern of activation in that massive network of dominos starts with some input (the first domino or set of dominoes that get knocked over) and ends with some output (the last domino or set of dominoes that are knocked over). In between there are many different paths that link input to output. A massive network of layers of the majority of the 4.5 million dominos responsible for the complex processing, integration, and modulation of inputs and outputs. We could call them inter-dominos, just like their neural example.

Let's move from our domino network back to our neural network. Our human neural network is massive! The human brain has some 86 billion neurons, about ten times the number of people on this planet. These 86 billion neurons in the human brain truly constitute a massive number. When compared to a gorilla (33 billion), a chimpanzee (22 billion), or a rhesus monkey (6 billion) a remarkable number, and when compared to the number of neurons in the brains of a dog or cat, about 530 million and 250 million respectively, a truly remarkable number. Before you get overly excited about humans winning this neuron-number game, a blue whale has a similar number of neurons as that of a human, a pilot whale has double the number, and an orca three times more. An elephant has even four times the number of neurons. Are elephants brainier, and therefore smarter? Perhaps. But their brains are much larger too.

More impressive and more important than the number of neurons is the number of neurons in one specific part of the human brain, the cerebral cortex[4]. The cerebral cortex is the outer layer of the brain in humans and other mammals and plays a key role in attention, perception, awareness, thought, memory, language, and consciousness. The cerebral cortex is the part of the brain responsible for cognition. In this area of the brain alone, humans have over 16 billion neurons. We easily recognize the human cortex by the so-called sulci and gyri, the grooves and ridges of the outer layer of the brain. The advantage of such a wrinkled outer brain is that it fits cortex the size of large newspaper in a relatively small skull (and any mother is grateful for such a wrinkled brain when their baby is in the process of being born). More of these convolutions in the cortex, more so-called sulci and gyri, have often been thought to be indicative of higher intelligence. This belief stemmed from comparisons of human brains to those of other animals. The logic here should become familiar. Human brains happen to have more cortical convolutions. And let's not forget that we must be smarter than other non-human animals! Therefore, more cortical convolutions simply must prove a smarter species. Had humans had an advanced *avian nido-pallium caudolaterale*, a specialized neural structure that processes visual information for navigation, I am sure that would prove why we are again so much smarter than other non-human animals. However, it is not humans who have an advanced *avian nidopallium caudolaterale* but pigeons who do – making them excel in navigation. Humans are simply self-centric when it comes to intelligence.

Nowadays, it is believed that the cortical folding in the cortex is linked to specific cognitive functions, and that drawing a direct relation between convolutions and higher cognition is too simple. The relationship is far more complex and multifaceted. Pretty much like intelligence is.

## HOW ARE HUMAN BRAINS COMPLEX?

The human brain's highly organized neural networks interact dynamically across different regions that specialize in different tasks. Albeit not exclusively so, each region is more or less responsible for processing different kinds of information, ranging from processing sensory input, executing motor control, or being particularly involved in memory functions.

To illustrate the complexity of the brain, let's take a brief brain tour[5]. The cerebral cortex is divided in two halves, called hemispheres. The left hemisphere is primarily involved in logical reasoning, language processing, mathematics, and analytical thinking. The right hemisphere is believed to be more involved in creativity, spatial awareness, visual and musical abilities, and holistic thought processing. The two hemispheres are connected by a large band of fibres that ensures communication between the hemispheres. That is important because had this band of fibres not been in place, we would almost literally experience two worlds separately. The two hemispheres are cross wired: the left hemisphere controls the right side of our body (eyes, ears, arms, legs etc.), the right hemisphere the left side. Even though the hemispheres are specialized, they work in tandem, so as to provide a coherent understanding of the world. Claiming that somebody is a left-brainer or a right-brainer (and how to become a left-brainer or right-brainer) may be interesting to keep a party conversation going, but is not at all based on scientific evidence.

Each of our two hemispheres can be subdivided into four lobes. Each lobe is somewhat – but again not exclusively – specialized. On the very back of our head, we can find the occipital lobe, which houses the visual cortex. The visual cortex gets activated when we look at things. But it also lights up in language tasks, because we seem to visualize information. In fact, the visual cortex is activated in blind people too. The parietal lobe in front of the occipital lobe consists of a motor cortex and a sensory cortex, the somatosensory cortex. When we decide to move our arm, the motor cortex gets activated, when we touch that hot cup of coffee the sensory cortex gets activated. The temporal lobes on the side are for hearing and memory. In the left temporal lobe language areas can be found, such as Broca's area and Wernicke's area. In Wernicke's area the semantics, or meaning, of language gets processed, whereas in Broca's area, the syntax or language structure is processed. Finally, the frontal lobes located around your forehead are for planning and movement. The frontal lobes are particularly interesting for cognition. The part of the frontal cortex right at the top of your head is responsible for motor movement. The neurons at this part have a direct connection to the spinal cord to control muscle movement. More at the front of the frontal cortex lies the prefrontal cortex. The prefrontal cortex is responsible for attention, planning and keeping ideas in mind. The prefrontal cortex occupies 30% of the human brain, and for long it has been thought that it is the sheer size of the prefrontal cortex that makes us thinking animals. More recent evidence shows that it is the complexity and organization of neural circuits that makes humans 'unique'[6].

Beneath the lobes and the cerebral cortex lie several structures that handle more specialized tasks. For instance, the basal ganglia are responsible for planning movement and producing that movement, but also handle motivating behaviour. The thalamus, the control centre of the brain receives and organizes sensory information and relays it to the cerebral cortex. The hypothalamus, another control centre that regulates body temperature, blood pressure, and glucose levels and plays a role in thirst, hunger, aggression and lust. And the hippocampus and the amygdala, the former responsible for formation of the memories, the latter for associating emotions. More deeply hidden in the brain are the brain stem, controlling the most basic functions such as breathing, swallowing, and heart rate, and the cerebellum, the balance centre of the brain, important for allowing us to stand and coordinate our limbs. Evolutionarily, the organization of the brain is fascinating. The most basic functions of the brain critical for our survival lie hidden, deep inside of the brain, almost on top of the spinal cord. At least two aspects are intriguing here. First, evolution has apparently taken care of the most vital function being most protected against injury. If our cerebral cortex gets damaged, we may not be able to plan, pay attention or keep ideas in our mind, but at least we will survive. Second, over time, subcortical structures have been built on top of the vital ones. If we take this to an extreme, we could argue that breathing and heart rate are more important than memory and emotions, which are more important than control of movement and motivation, which are more important than thinking. Thinking basically is a nice-to-have but not really a must-have. In terms of survival at least.

As I mentioned earlier, the outer layer of neural tissue of the brain in humans and other mammals is the cerebral cortex, the part of the brain responsible for cognition, for thinking. To demonstrate the complexity of the human brain in general and the cortex in particular, a study by a group of molecular and cellular biologists speaks volumes[7]. They mapped out a 3D cubic millimetre (.04 inch) of human temporal cortex at extremely high resolution. That one very tiny piece of brain tissue contained about 57,000 cells, about 230 millimetres of blood vessels, and about 150 million synapses, the connections between the neurons. Moreover, that tiny piece of brain tissue comprised an astonishing 1.4 petabytes of data! To store that amount of data would require about 1,000 large home computers! One can only imagine how many computers would be needed for an artificial brain to replicate the complexity of the human brain! It is high time to have a look at an artificial brain.

## HOW DO ARTIFICIAL BRAINS THINK?

In case you started to think this book was turning out to be more about neuroscience than about artificial intelligence, let me reassure you that you are still reading the same book on the same topic. But understanding the complexity of the human brain is helpful for understanding artificial intelligence. The architecture of the human brain, the millions of years of evolution of the human brain, and the way information travels through the brain in patterns of activation is helpful in understanding artificial brains. Not the ones that are located in the heads of human-like robots, but artificial brains that form the architectures that make machines think. The very architecture of what creates artificial intelligence. And you are right. Just as the notion of flying does not need to consist of flapping wings like a bird, as artificial birds called airplanes demonstrate, the concept of thinking may need a neural network for human minds, but not necessarily for artificial minds. Artificial brains do not need to look like human brains. And yet the history of artificial intelligence has shown that the human brain has served as a very useful example in the advancement of artificial intelligence. Another example of understanding artificial minds through humans minds. Another example of the psychology of AI!

These days it has become very difficult to think of artificial intelligence without thinking of artificial neural networks. In fact, today's most impressive accomplishments in artificial intelligence come from artificial neural networks. They have also been called parallel distributed systems because they operate in parallel rather than in sequence. Or connectionist networks, because their many connections between interconnected nodes. These days they are more commonly known as models of *deep learning*. Because these models of deep learning are so essential to artificial intelligence, it is worthwhile to understand their mechanisms. However, that turns out to be a challenge without the mathematics and computer science behind it, so bear with me.

Imagine a pile of sand. The one you can scoop with your own hands on the beach. That pile of sand is pretty much a metaphorical blank slate with no patterns until you pour some water over the pile. Initially, the water flows in all kinds of directions with no noticeable patterns. Over time however, the more water gets poured over the pile, channels form, and they appear to deepen with more water entering the network of channels. That water increasingly finds its way faster and faster through the channels that have been formed to stay. Slowly but surely a network of waterways starts channelling information (the water) in increasingly predictable directions. The input (the water being poured), finds the output (the bottom of the pile of sand) through patterns of water activation. If this example does not make any sense, I really recommend you take a break and (preferably accompanied by this book) spend a day at the beach.

Let's now imagine that the many channels in that pile of sand converge into one channel. Just before that final converging channel we place a dam that blocks the water. When enough water has been collected before the dam, but only then, we let the water through. The very first artificial neural network worked like this. It used logical rules such as AND (connecting two waterways), OR (choosing which of two waterways would let water through) and NOT (not allowing a waterway to let water through) to let the water flow through the channels of the network, illustrated by the arrow lines in the figure below.

As a graduate student, Marvin Minsky, later present at the 1956 Dartmouth Research Project on Artificial Intelligence as well as at the 1956 MIT Symposium that launched the cognitive revolution, was fascinated by the early mathematical models. Minsky and fellow physics student Dean Edmonds wondered whether they would be able to build an actual computer that could do this. With the help from psychologist George Miller – the one also present at the MIT symposium and who later created WordNet – they built one of the first electronic learning machines in 1951, with neurons and synapses and internal memory loops that simulated a rat in the network and set out to learn a path to some specified end point. With 3,000 vacuum tubes to simulate a network of 40 neurons the first maze-solving computer was created. Some five years later, psychologist Frank Rosenblatt developed the perceptron, an algorithm for pattern recognition, a mini-artificial neural network. Two things are important to keep in mind here. First, the perceptron, considered the first real artificial neural network for reasons explained in the next chapter, was developed around the time the term artificial intelligence was coined, and computer technology became more common. Second, artificial neural networks were not so much designed by computer scientists as they were by neuroscientists and psychologists, with an interest in computational implementations. By psychologists of artificial intelligence.

The problem with the early neural network models is that a pathway was either open or closed. Imagine two waterways that merge into one, waterway x might let a red dyed liquid through, waterway y a blue dyed liquid, which would create a red (NOT blue), a blue (NOT red) or a blue or red (red OR blue) outcome. In addition, when both waterways were open (red AND blue) a purple liquid may flow through the output channel. This model would have two input units and one output unit. But the options of the model are rather limited. Later models added an interesting complexity by building in a hidden waterway layer[8]. Let me explain. Combinations of three different colours (red, green and blue) mix into a range of different combinatory colours: red (red, no green, no blue), green (no red, green, no blue), blue (no red, no green, blue), purple (red, no green, blue), etc. But now let's say that we can change the width of the waterways. We don't just say that all red and all blue (or no red and only blue) can pass through, but a bit of red and a bit more blue. Now we use three funnels each taking a different colour, let's say red, green, and blue. Adjusting the width of the waterway, basically setting the weights with which an amount of coloured liquid is let through, we can create a variety of colour patterns. If we set the amount of liquid to a specific percentage, say 100% red, 50% green, and 0% blue, the colour orange emerges. With 0% red, 50% green and 100% blue the light blue colour of cyan comes out. As we have seen, 50% red, 100% blue and 0% green yields purple, and 50% of red, 50% of green and 50% of blue turns into grey.

These combinatory orange, cyan, purple, and grey can be combined in two pathways that yield – depending on the weights set to the pathways – two output colour units (light green and lavender). Note that if we look at the entire neural network, we see three input colours, four intermediate colours that lead to two output colours. Or actually, we see three input colours that result in two output colours (light green and lavender) through different combinations (including a layer of orange, cyan, purple and grey colours). But when focusing on the input and the output, that intermediate layer does not really matter, it is hidden.

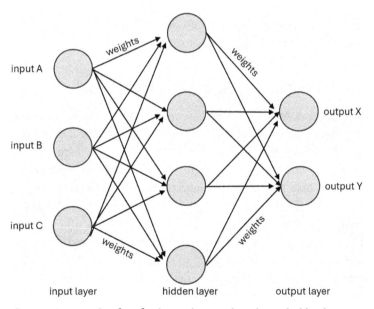

**Figure 4.1** Example of artificial neural network with one hidden layer.

Artificial neural networks are obviously more complex than the example here, and have become much more complex over the years. The example above only has one hidden layer, whereas an architecture such as GPT-4 has over 96 and DeepSeek 61 hidden layers! But in essence the structure of these sophisticated models is similar to the simple (waterways) model presented here.

Basically, an artificial neural network is like a very (very!) simplified version of the human neural network in the human brain. In an input layer, input units get their information, pretty much like the sensory neurons in the human brain. Each input unit sends the distributed information – the $1 - 0 - 1 - 1 - 0 - 1 - 1 - 1 - 0 - 1$ if the artificial neural network had ten input units – to the hidden layer, the first of many or the only one. The hidden layer of the neural network distributes the information further by figuring out patterns of information. When the hidden layer has (or layers have) distributed features of information across the network, an output layer gives the final result. As if dyed water poured in different input units forms patterns of water over the pile of sand through hidden layers, ultimately leading to a colour combination.

## HOW ARE ARTIFICIAL BRAINS COMPLEX?

The accomplishments of the most recent artificial neural networks are astonishing, and so is their architecture. And yet the most sophisticated artificial neural network does not come anywhere near the complexity of the human brain. The 86 billion neurons in the human brain can have thousands of connections to other neurons, leading to trillions of synapses. Even though we need to be careful not to make one-to-one mappings between human and artificial brains, the impressive GPT-4 only has around 100 layers, and each layer only contains thousands of units, so that it only has hundreds of billions of connections. When it comes to human and artificial brains, human brains win the number game.

But it is not only the numbers that distinguish the neural networks in human minds and artificial minds. The description of the process with which neurons in the human brain communicate with each other seems to be very crisp and clear. Reality, however, is different. Neurons are considered very noisy, in the sense that there is considerable variability and randomness in the signals neurons produce. This is even the case when neurons are exposed to the exact same stimulus repeatedly. Apparently, there is room for variation when neurons in the human brain communicate. Artificial neural networks on the other hand leave no room for variability. They are deterministic: given the same input, they will produce the same output each and every time[9].

This chapter started out describing the complexity of the brain: the different parts of the brain and their different functions. All the parts of the brain, however, work together, whereas for artificial neural networks this is not the case. They can be somewhat specialized by the layers or their general architecture, but there is no multifunctionality. Different tasks are handled by different artificial neural networks with different specific architectures. Architectures like Recurrent Neural Networks (RNNs) or Transformers (such as GPT and DeepSeek) excel at handling sequential information, and are therefore very good at speech and language processing. Similar to the left temporal lobe in the human brain. Convolutional Neural Networks (CNNs) on the other hand excel at analysing images by processing visual data in hierarchical stages, recognizing simple patterns like edges before merging them into more complex shapes and objects. This is akin to how the occipital lobe in the human brain processes visual stimuli. The very fact that these artificial neural networks are currently task-specific makes the idea of Artificial General Intelligence (AGI) akin to the accomplishments of the human brain still very much something of the future. At least for now.

## HOW ARE ARTIFICIAL BRAINS BIOLOGICALLY PLAUSIBLE?

Artificial neural networks have biological plausibility. Had they not, this chapter would obviously not have devoted its first half to the description of the human brain and its mechanisms. Indeed, the structural and functional properties of artificial neural networks are very similar to their human example. They are both composed of individual units that function like neurons, that receive inputs, process them, and send outputs to other units, creating complex networks that can process information. Both systems have a layered structure with relatively few input units, relatively few output units and a very large number of interneurons. Both process multiple pieces of information at the same time, and both use information that is distributed across the network rather than being stored in a single location. Evolution of the human brain has demonstrated that such an architecture is great for thinking.

One of the major advantages of parallel distributed processing is that neural networks are robust. If we take the pile-of-sand metaphor as an example for both human and artificial neural networks, imagine the following. One of the pathways gets blocked, for instance because a pathway unexpectedly gets caved in when part of the pile of sand collapses. For the distributed information in the network, a blocked pathway is not ideal as patterns of activation have stabilized the network. But the clever architecture makes this accident not a disastrous one, because the information is distributed. Other pathways can relatively easily compensate for the blocked pathway. In psychology, these blocked pathways have a dedicated name: a stroke. When a brain attack occurs, the blood supply to parts of the brain gets blocked. Although it depends on the extent of the stroke, the extent to which the parts of the pile of sand caved in, often the network recovers relatively well and only minor damage remains. Initially the damage seems very severe, but over time other parts of the network take over. Water gets re-distributed over the pathways, just like neural networks re-create and re-distribute patterns of activation. The same is true for artificial neural networks. If a pathway in the network happens to collapse (for instance because a computational glitch happens to set the wrong weight in one of the pathways), the system can still function relatively well.

Another example of the robustness of the network is not so much related to the architecture of the network, as it is to the nature of the information. Imagine again our waterways example. We pour the dyed liquid in the input units, but spill. Too much red and too little blue are poured over the pile of sand, more and less than we had really intended. Because the distributed nature of the network, the networks is able to reconstruct information even if the information is suboptimal or missing. Basically, once the pathways of the network have been formed, the model 'knows' how to distribute the information over the architecture. The input may be incomplete, and yet the output can be as complete as before. Thanks to these many distributed patterns between input and output. You may see only part of the picture, only hear fragments of the speech, only have the smell of the item in question, and you will still be able to reconstruct the entire concept.

Because so many pathways carry bits and pieces of information it also means that the performance of the network decays gradually rather than suddenly. Had there been only one pathway, the information would be all there or all gone. But in a parallel distributed network pieces of information will be retained. For instance, in the aging human brain, information does not easily get destroyed. Only bits of distributed information are chipped of. With some remaining additional distributed information, a thought can be reconstructed again. It might take a bit longer, but the reconstruction process will most likely be successful. You don't remember the name of that old friend of yours? Patterns of activation help you to get there (imagining her face, remembering where she lived, what she was wearing, where you met).

That network of distributed representations also allows for dealing with new information. If we return to the waterways metaphor, there is a very large range of different pathways with each node in the pathway allowing for being set to different weights so that a range of different colours – well beyond the ones illustrated here – become possible. So, pouring over an entirely different colour of liquid, might get you to some very creative solutions, very new because of the new colours but not entirely unfamiliar because of the pathways that have been formed.

There is also a sustainability advantage. By distributing information, we do not need to have dedicated pathways but can have pathways that are reused with pieces of information. In the waterways metaphor, we do not need a pathway dedicated to orange, cyan, purple, grey, light green and lavender, the pathways different combinations of pathways and weights will do the trick. Relatedly, neural networks process information in a parallel distributed fashion. Information (water in our examples) travels through the network at the same time, rather than in sequence. A distributed model thereby saves memory resources. There is no colour orange, there is a combination of pathways that make the colour orange. That means that we can get to orange through the red colour, but also through the green colour.

Before we get carried away by dominos, waterways, and biological plausibility, let's not forget there are some major differences between artificial and human neural networks. The human brain has approximately 86 billion neurons and trillions of connections (synapses) in that sense very much outperforming the most sophisticated artificial neural network. But the brain's complexity also arises from the vast biochemical processes, synaptic plasticity, and dynamic wiring of its neurons, which have no true parallel in artificial neural networks. In fact, one may argue that the early artificial neural networks may have been a very simplified representation of the human brain, but over time, deep learning models have become less biologically plausible, because the emphasis started to shift from biological plausible to computational manageable. When considering today's artificial neural networks with their unique computational structures, perhaps there no longer is a psychology of artificial intelligence, because there does not need to be. Even then, historical, terminological and conceptual reasons warrant the comparison between the two.

Artificial neural networks are a very simplified model of the human neural network. A very simplified version indeed. Even though artificial neural networks are inspired by the structure and function of the human brain, they differ in many ways. Biological brains are multifunctional. They can process all kinds of information simultaneously. You can see a venomous snake, start getting scared, remember the last time you saw a snake, and make the decision to act and run away. All pretty much at the same time. Artificial neural networks are task-specific, they can pretty much do one thing at the time, and one network cannot do different things. Instead, they are highly specialized, making Artificial General Intelligence, the intelligence of a human neural network, an artificial intelligence goal for the future. The distant or not so distant future.

## HOW IS KNOWLEDGE REPRESENTED IN HUMAN AND ARTIFICIAL BRAINS?

Knowledge representation has been illustrated as dyed liquid poured over a pile of sand. Hardly a real topic in cognitive psychology. Towards the end of this chapter, could we please get an actual example from cognitive psychology? One that is not an illustration, but an actual example.

In the 1960s, psychologist Ross Quillian worked on a computer that 'understands'[10]. Quillian built a knowledge base that represented semantic relations between concepts in a network, a form of knowledge representation, a WordNet *avant la lettre*. Quillian proposed that knowledge in human and artificial minds may be organized in hierarchical networks, fixed, tree-like structures where more specific concepts are nested under more general ones. A database with information tells us that a canary is a bird, and a bird is an animal. For each node in the hierarchical network, features can be identified; for instance, that canaries can sing and that they are yellow. That birds have wings and can fly. And that animals eat, breathe and can move. In this example we have distinguished three levels of information: a superordinate level category (animal), a basic level category (bird) and a subordinate category (canary). Psychology experiments demonstrated evidence for these three levels in the hierarchy. When participants were asked to list features for each of these three levels, most features were given for basic level categories, most likely because this level is more informative than the subordinate level, yet more distinctive than the superordinate level[11]. At the same time, evidence demonstrated that participants were fastest in categorizing concepts as a superordinate level compared to the basic or subordinate level.

These hierarchical networks are a good example of what I called Symbolic AI in the previous chapter, good old-fashioned AI. The problem with hierarchical networks as knowledge representation is the rigidity in structure. For instance, just like a canary a penguin is a bird, but one that does not fly. Perhaps the hierarchical network needs to consist of a category of animals that consists of birds, and within the category birds there are flying birds (with canaries as a member) and non-flying birds (with penguins as a category). But what to do with a canary whose wings are injured so that it can no longer fly? But the hierarchical network suffers from additional problems that are well beyond canaries and penguins too. What to do with tomatoes, that are considered fruits and vegetables? Or where do abstract concepts such freedom and justice fit the network?

Psychologist Eleanor Rosch argued that instead of using hierarchies, human minds and artificial minds organize and categorize information based on prototypes. By using prototypical examples, hierarchical classifications would move toward more flexible, graded categories. A penguin may still be a bird, but not a prototypical one. A robin on the other hand might be considered a prototype because it closely matches our mental image of a typical bird. The prototype theory helped to shift the understanding of how humans categorize the world, moving away from strict rule-based models to more flexible, experience-based models. But despite the advantages of a prototype theory compared to a hierarchical network, the prototype theory suffered from very similar problems. There's no strict rule for determining whether a penguin is still a bird; and how does it compare to an ostrich? And what is the prototype for freedom and justice? Despite being more flexible than the hierarchical network theory, the prototype theory turned out to still be too rigid. Good, perhaps better, but still good old-fashioned AI.

In the mid 1970s, psychologists Alan Collins and Elizabeth Loftus solved the problems with hierarchical networks and prototype theories as knowledge representation by proposing a network of associations, whereby an item is defined by distinctive features which are linked to other items. The Spreading Activation Theory. *Penguin* and *bird* were associated by the distinctive features of *wing*, and *beak* but not by *flying*. But *flying* in turn links *bird* to *airplane*, and to *Tweety*, which also links the colour *yellow* to *school bus* (but not to *airplane* or *bird* or *penguin* unless they happen to yellow). The activation of one feature would activate other nodes in the network. Such an associative network architecture would allow for retrieving information faster. Rather than traversing a hierarchical graph structure, it would be possible to infer relationships. Just like in human minds, I may think of a canary not because of the fact it is a bird, but because I was thinking of a cat or a cage, or a Warner Brothers cartoon. It could place penguins in patterns that are similar to birds but not quite. Red canaries that can neither sing nor fly, can still fit well in the network. The network would even allow for creating new concepts that do not exist. One where there is room for creativity, whereby purple canaries with trunks that bark can roam around in the network space.

Having been introduced to artificial neural networks, you may notice the similarities between the Spreading Activation Theory and artificial neural networks. Activation of semantic information such as *beak*, *fly*, or *wings*, spread through the network of knowledge associations like dyed liquid. Knowledge representations in terms of rule-based systems such as those in hierarchical networks have important advantages: if an item and the rule are part of the network, it will get you to the exact right information. But scaling up such networks is tedious and if an item is not part of the network the rule-based system fails. An alternative to hierarchical networks, a prototype theory, solves the rigidity problem by allowing categories to have graded memberships. Some items are more typical or central to a category reflecting how human minds often categorize concepts in a flexible, experience-based way. The prototype theory can be seen as fuzzy logic, which also deals with graded membership by assigning degrees of truth between 0 and 1. It handles situations where something can partially belong to multiple categories. However, just as fuzzy logic had difficulties to scale up, prototype theory did not quite scale up. Associations would provide the solution. Collins and Loftus, however, developed their model to explain human memory and semantic retrieval in cognitive psychology. Their model meanwhile influenced artificial intelligence because it reflected the flexibility and adaptivity the neural networks of human and artificial minds characterize.

The notion of knowledge representation in a parallel distributed processing network, an artificial neural network, has not only been appealing theoretically. In practice, it has shown great advantages for cognitive psychology and artificial intelligence[12]. In fact, it has played a major role in understanding how human and artificial minds understand language, as we will see later.

Now at the very end of this chapter I have a confession to make. I have described human and artificial minds in terms of human and artificial neural networks. I tried to do this without mathematical and computational terminology and have tried to be complete. But in the description of the architecture of human and artificial minds I left out one important, one very critical component of artificial neural networks. The very component that makes neural networks, human and artificial ones, so powerful in their flexibility and adaptivity. It is a major omission on my end. The bad news is that this component was left out of the current chapter. The good news is that it will feature a central role in the next chapter.

# 5

## HOW DO HUMAN AND ARTIFICIAL MINDS LEARN?

For a human or artificial brain to be considered intelligent more is needed than to solely process information; more is needed than to pass on input to output through a neural network. After all, if all there were to reasoning and thinking is regurgitating the same information in the same way over and over again, human and artificial minds need to be downgraded to the functioning of a calculator with the same input always leading to the exact same output. Instead, for human and artificial minds to be considered intelligent, they ought to be able to adapt and to learn.[1]

### HOW DO HUMAN MINDS LEARN?

The newborn brain is about a quarter of the size of an adult brain. Yet the newborn brain has only a slightly lower number of neurons than the fully developed adult brain. These neurons are mostly formed during foetal development. The big difference in the newborn brain when compared with an adult brain is not the number of neurons, but the extremely high density of synapses, the connections between the neurons. At birth, each neuron has already formed thousands of connections, so much so that a newborn brain has 1 quadrillion neural connections at birth, compared to the "meagre"

DOI: 10.4324/9781003491095-5

100 to 500 trillion synapses adults have. What happened? It turns out that the many connections of the newborn brain are pruned over time with connections that are not needed, losing their worth. The adult brain basically becomes gradually more and more specialized. The not-so-specialized-newborn-brain on the other hand has one major advantage. Because of the very high number of connections, it is highly flexible and adaptable to the environment. It is basically all geared up to learn.

When we look at the neural level, learning consists of neurons making connections with one another. They fire and wire. The idea was introduced by psychologist Donald Hebb[2], and is commonly known as Hebbian Learning[3]. Hebb argued that if neurons fire together, they wire together. Think about it. When you learn a particular behaviour, say you are a baby learning how to walk, initially the steps you take are very deliberate. You are very conscious of where and how you place your feet. You fall, stand up, and are very aware of what you do. To state this extremely (and extremely) simplistically, no neurons are wired yet, because no neurons fired yet. Over time, however, network connections are formed that allow you to think less of these initial steps you take. The behaviour becomes very automatic. Neurons that are fired together become wired connections, so that what seemed difficult and deliberate becomes easy and automatic. Practice makes perfect.

If you are not quite convinced about this automatic behaviour, try hopscotch. When you first learned how to do hopscotch when you were a child, you carefully thought about where to place your one foot, then the next. But if you try hopscotch now, it has become an automatic behaviour. If it has not, you may have to learn it again in order for it to become an automatic behaviour. Still not convinced? Try walking down the stairs, I presume an automatic behaviour. Now let's undo the automatic behaviour and think of every movement you make. What your toes are doing, how you land your feet, how you take the next step. When you do, you trip and fall (and I therefore recommend leaving this example only as a thought experiment exercise).

Hebbian learning nicely illustrates how the overabundance of synapses in the newborn brain get pruned to a more specialized neural network when we become older. Use it or lose it, when it comes to those synaptic connections. If you recall the waterways illustration from the previous chapter, connections in the pile of sand get stronger when water flows through it – water flows faster over time when pathways are used. At the same time, pathways that remain unused because no water flows through them slowly but surely disappear.

That is learning at the neural level, but what about learning at the psychological level? The learning as we know it. Most psychologists define this kind of learning as "a relatively enduring change in behaviour resulting from experience."[4] What would be needed in this process of learning is a focusing on relevant information while filtering out distractions (what we call attention). And we need to combine this with an ability to encode, store, and retrieve information (what we call memory). As well as a response that tells us what our performance output is in order to help refine skills and correct mistakes (what we call feedback). Let's dive into some types of learning that are distinguished in psychology.

When we think of learning, the most obvious kind of learning most of us think of is what is called "explicit learning", the deliberate learning when we are acquiring knowledge or skills. This is the kind of learning that takes place at schools. Through formal instruction, and with effort and attention, we follow lectures, study for exams, and participate in tutorials. Or so do teachers and professors hope. In the words of my daughter on a Monday morning: "Off to another week at work. A hard day's work!" In this type of learning we know what needs to be learned. The learning material has been labelled to be learned. And over time we have learned enough for our learning performance to be tested.

A second type of learning comes automatic to us. It is the kind of learning where we learn by doing. We pick up patterns in the real world, make associations, and without being really aware of it, we master the learning material. A good example of this type of learning, implicit learning, is the acquisition of language. Well before they go to school children acquire language and are not explicitly taught how to do this. It just happens over time. Children hear language and start to copy it, recognize patterns and use these patterns in their own language production. Initially they make errors but over time children prune their language productions to wonderful grammatical sentences. This automatic learning is the complete opposite of explicit learning and it is therefore called implicit learning.

Both implicit and explicit learning can take place in a type of learning most familiar to psychology students[5]. This type of learning started with Russian experimental neurologist and physiologist Ivan Pavlov, who received a Nobel Prize for his work on digestion in dogs (and not so much for introducing this type of learning). In order to determine how food affected the salivary glands in the dogs' mouths, Pavlov developed a small device that was implanted surgically in a dog's mouth to collect its saliva. A dog would salivate when it saw a bowl of its favourite food. This is not very surprising if you yourself think about your mouth-watering favourite food. But Pavlov then noticed that a dog would also salivate when it only heard the footsteps of a lab assistant delivering the food. Apparently the dog had associated the footsteps with the bowl of food and because the food made the dog salivate, the footsteps now also had it salivate in anticipation of a delicious meal. The participant of the experiment (the dog), had learned to associate an unconditioned stimulus (food) with an unconditioned response (salivating). Each time the lab assistant walked to the dog to deliver the food, the dog learned to associate the unconditioned stimulus with a conditioned stimulus (the latter being the footsteps that would initially not yield the dog to salivate), so that over time only the conditioned stimulus (the footsteps) yielded a conditioned response (the salivation).

Psychologist John Watson showed how classical conditioning also affected humans. Not by focusing on salivation, but by focusing on emotions. The best example is the experiment with Little Albert. Eleven-month-old Albert was perfectly fine when a white rat hopped around him. In fact, he was delighted seeing any white furry animal. However, Watson made the rat became a conditioned stimulus, when each time the rat appeared a loud clanging sound was produced. The unconditioned clanging sound scared Albert and made him cry. By associating the white rat to the loud clanging noise, the white rat too made Albert scared. So scared that the association generalized to all white furry animals, and even to Santa Claus with his white furry beard.

The unexpected discovery by Pavlov and the subsequent findings by Watson turned out to be revolutionary. Psychologist B.F. Skinner was very much influenced by Pavlov and Watson. Even today Skinner is considered the most eminent psychologist of the 20th century, according to the American Psychological Association[6]. Skinner felt that the classical conditioning of pairing a stimulus to a biological response (salivation or other reflexes that one cannot stop, such as crying to a clanging noise), would only explain automatic behaviour. But often we learn behaviour that is not automatic. According to Skinner, most learning takes place by having an organism actively being involved in the consequences of its behaviour. Skinner used rats and pigeons as participants in his experiments (but he could have chosen salivating dogs or humans delighted to see white furry animals). These rat and pigeon participants learned to press a lever to receive food. The rats or pigeons were placed in a box with a lever. When the animal pressed the lever, food would appear. First, the animal in the Skinner box would be just moving around until it by accident hit the lever. The moment the lever was pressed, food was delivered on a food tray. Initially the animal must have thought the food was delivered accidentally, but over time it learned how to get rewarded for pressing the lever.

Skinner took these discoveries further by shaping the behaviour of an animal. A pigeon would stand in front of Skinner and accidentally made a move to the right. The moment this happened the pigeon was rewarded with food. If it accidentally moved to the left nothing happened, but when it moved to the right again the food appeared. You get the idea. Over time, slowly but surely, the pigeon learned how to make a pirouette by being reinforced to perform a particular behaviour. It was not taught to make a pirouette, nobody whispered in some uncoded pigeon language that the bird needed to make a pirouette. Instead, the pigeon learned the behaviour by being reinforced.

If the pigeon pressed a lever, food would be delivered. The food acted as a reward, reinforcing the behaviour of pecking behaviour. Increasing the pecking behaviour could also be obtained in a different albeit less enjoyable way. The pigeon could also be placed in a chamber while mild shocks would be administered to the poor little bird. The moment the animal pecked the lever, the shocks would stop. Here not the adding of a stimulus (the food) but the removing of a stimulus (the shock) would reinforce the key-pecking behaviour. Reversely, if the experimenter wanted a pigeon to stop pecking the key, it could provide a punishment (a shock or an otherwise aversive stimulus) so that the animal would less likely repeat the behaviour. Or the animal abandoned the key pecking behaviour by food being stopped to be administered. These four conditions (positive reinforcement by providing food, negative reinforcement by removing shocks, positive punishments by delivering shocks and negative punishment by removing food) would explain pretty much all animal behaviour according to Skinner. Including the behaviour of human animals.

Explicit learning and implicit learning. Operant conditioning whereby the participant is reinforced to conduct a particular behaviour. A crash course on the chapter of learning in human minds that helps understand learning in artificial minds.

## HOW DO ARTIFICIAL MINDS LEARN?

Remember the earlier definition of learning for human minds: "A relatively enduring change in behaviour resulting from experience." Let's apply that definition to artificial minds. According to computer scientist Tom Mitchell,[7] the definition of machine learning is as follows: "A computer program is said to learn from experience E with respect to some class of tasks T and performance measure P if its performance at tasks in T, as measured by P, improves with experience E." That is, machine learning is the kind of learning by computers whereby the performance on a specific task improves with experience.

The term "machine learning" was coined in 1959, that's right, only three years after the term "artificial intelligence" was coined. And almost a decade after Donald Hebb proposed what we now know as Hebbian learning. It was the time of Skinner's operant conditioning – Skinner who Donald Hebb stated to regard as the greatest psychologist of the century, and who must undoubtedly have influenced Hebb's work. It was more than a decade after the first mathematical model of a neural network, almost a decade after the first artificial neural network using 3,000 vacuum tubes to simulate a network of 40 neurons. And it was a year before the perceptron was developed, the early mini-artificial neural network with a hidden layer. When learning was a hot topic in psychology, machine learning became a hot topic in artificial intelligence.

But for artificial minds to learn stuff – not to regurgitate but to actually learn – is easier said than done. Human minds are equipped for learning, babies with their 1 quadrillion neural connections particularly. But machines need somebody, not a parent but a programmer, to tell them exactly what to do. A programmer who lays out every part of the machine learning process. When and what to eat (most commonly data), when and how to walk (from a simple beep to a football playing robot) and when and how to talk (from a Google search to a generative AI chatbot).

What you should have learned by now (no pun intended!), is that when confronted with a question in artificial intelligence, the answer to that question can be found in psychology. This is no different for the question of how artificial minds learn.

## HOW DO ARTIFICIAL MINDS USE SUPERVISED LEARNING?

The most intuitive type of (human) learning, the one we are most familiar with after years of school, is explicit learning. An example of explicit learning is where the learner (the human student) learns items from a memory list. As is the case in learning a foreign language: word items for one language are learned for the other language. The input is clear. The English word "dog" is the French *chien*, the English word "cat" is the French *chat*. The output is also clear: when the word "dog" is given to the human learner, the French word *chien* is expected when the learning process is completed. All the input data is labelled ("dog" consists of the label *chien*), and the human learner learns from the labelled input data and can produce output data. Somebody, a teacher or supervisor, labelled the input data and checks the accuracy of the answers in the output data.

Supervised learning in machines works in the same way. What is called explicit learning in human minds is aptly called "supervised learning" in artificial minds. In supervised learning, a computer model is trained to get us from input data to the desired output, also known as a human-labelled supervisory signal. The process is supervised: the input data is labelled, and the output data can be checked by the supervisor (the machine).

To demonstrate how supervised learning works, rather than asking a machine to learn that the French word for "dog" is *chien* (which would literally be one line of code that the machine will never mess up on), let's consider a machine that learns how to distinguish between actual emails and spam emails. You are undoubtedly familiar with them, the ones you probably receive on a daily basis. The ones where you were awarded billionaire status because some prince somewhere in the world inherited you a large sum of money (if only you would pay the sender of the email some transfer fees). Or the ones where you only need to click that button to obtain your prize (if only you enter the click-bait). Imagine that we want to develop a machine learning algorithm that aims to distinguish whether an email is genuine or spam. Basically, we are trying to develop a spam filter.

Let's say that we take 3,000 emails from our inbox. For now, we save 1,000 emails for later and first work with 2,000 of these emails. Notice here that we are talking about *supervised learning* here. The emails have been labelled in advance whether they are genuine or spam. Let's assume that one part of our machine learning algorithm is to break down the email into words. The machine learning model here applies feature extraction, breaking down the raw material (the emails) into features (the words). When it does this for all 2,000 emails, we end up with an imaginary spreadsheet with one column consisting of all the unique words in all 2,000 emails, both genuine and spam emails. In a second and third column in the imaginary spreadsheet the system now marks whether a word occurred in a genuine or in a spam email respectively. For instance, the second column finds a frequency greater than null particularly for "dear", "will", "thanks", "regards" (because these happen to be the words in the genuine emails). The third column marks a frequency greater than null for "dear", "prince", "inheritance", "prize" and "click", "regards". Once our machine learning algorithm has processed all the emails, it is trained to identify which of all the features in all emails (Column 1) are responsible for genuine (Column 2) versus spam (Column 3) emails. Our machine learning algorithm has learned that when an email consists of "prince", "inheritance", "prize" and "click" it has a much higher probability of being spam.

"Duh!" you might exclaim. "You had data that was labelled as genuine, or spam, and you are now able to identify whether that data is genuine or spam. Impressive learning for an artificial mind. Call that intelligence...!" Just like the human mind learns English and French words in a memory list, the magic does not so much lie in the training phase of the machine learning. In the training phase the mind is allowed to make mistakes, just like you are allowed to make mistakes in learning the translation of the word "dog" in French. The magic lies elsewhere, in the testing phase. In the training phase, it already is remarkable that the machine has automatically learned which features allow it to classify the input data into genuine or spam.

The accomplishments in machine learning really start when the machine learning model gets assessed. After the supervised learning in a training phase, we can now measure how good the model is in a testing phase. In that phase the machine learning model gets new, unseen data. That data is still labelled behind the scenes, but in the testing phase the algorithm is not allowed to peak at the labelled data. That also means that it cannot extract *new* features as it did in the training phase, but can only apply the *learned* features. And be tested.

The training phase in machine learning assumes working with a representative data set. In the spam filter example, the model has extracted all the words from all the emails, both genuine and spam emails, and assumes these are all the words that ever appear in genuine and spam emails. If there happened to be words in the emails in the testing dataset that were not in the training dataset, the model would simply not know what to do with these words. The dataset for training is therefore always larger than the data set for testing. Typically, 70% of the data set is used for training and 30% is used for testing.

In this example we trained our supervised learning algorithm on 2,000 emails, half of them being genuine the other half being spam. We now take the 1,000 emails we left out from the training set, random emails the model has not seen yet. But emails of which the "supervisor" – it is supervised learning after all – happens to know whether these are genuine or spam emails. The machine now classifies these 1,000 emails and makes a decision by putting each email in the genuine or spam category. And it does it well. Let's say with 80% accuracy. The machine learned the features that distinguish the dataset between the categories that were labelled, and is then able to apply the algorithm to a new dataset it has never seen before. In this example we have seen that it can correctly classify 8 of 10 emails as genuine or spam. If we now let our learning algorithm go out in the wild, investigate every incoming email, we can predict with 80% accuracy that the system is able to filter out the unwanted emails from our emails.

## HOW DO ARTIFICIAL MINDS USE UNSUPERVISED LEARNING?

Just like implicit learning is the opposite of explicit learning, so is unsupervised learning the opposite of supervised learning. The advantage of unsupervised learning is that no labelled data are needed. The machine learning process decides itself what category a data point is placed in. From the ground up, data-driven, it creates clusters of similar data. This of course saves a lot of time and effort. No supervisor needs to go through the dataset and label the data. In our email dataset example, nobody needs to go through the thousands of emails and mark "genuine", "spam", "spam", "genuine", a rather tedious and boring exercise. That's the upside. The downside of unsupervised learning is that we simply do not know what categories the machine learning algorithm will come up with.

Take our earlier example of the thousands of emails. In unsupervised learning we can ask the machine learning algorithm to come with clusters of emails. It basically discovers categories for us. The algorithm finds hidden patterns or intrinsic structures in the data. Let's assume that the algorithm takes our email dataset and again breaks it down into words, and places these words in our imaginary spreadsheet. However, this time we do not know how many columns the machine learning algorithm should use. Basically, the different emails shoot out in every dimension. It is the system's task to find patterns in these dimensions. To apply some kind dimensionality reduction, to make the number of dimensions manageable.

Of all the emails in the dataset the system encounters, it finds that there is a group of emails consisting of the words "dear", "will", "thanks", "regards" with a frequency greater than null, but those emails never use the words "prince", "inheritance", "prize" or "click". There is also a group of emails that have a peculiar pattern. They vary in the words they use, but always contain the words "prince" and "inheritance" but never the words "prize" or "click". And then there are the emails with "prize" or "click" but never the words "prince" and "inheritance". All the other words in those emails vary. Based on the patterns our machine learning algorithm has discovered, it is now able to reduce the thousands of dimensions the emails shoot out to, back to three dimensions, three clusters, three categories. The machine learning algorithm has learned in an unsupervised fashion that our email dataset consists of a group of emails with varying words, a group with "prince" and "inheritance", and a group with "click" and "prize". The machine learning algorithm can give us the certainty with which it is able to get to these clusters (in this example that estimate would be rather high), what is called the *cluster purity*. What the system is not able to do is tell us what those categories are. It tells us that there are clusters, and which emails fall in these clusters, but it does not tell us what these clusters mean. That is up to us humans. In this example we might have a mixed group (let's call this group *Genuine*), a prince-inheritance group (let's call this group *Spam1*) and a click-bait group (let's call this group *Spam2*).

Making up simple examples is much easier than dealing with actual data. In the example we were able to identify specific words. But often the patterns the unsupervised machine learning algorithm discovers might be confusing or obscure. The system may have found word combinations that occur with some other word combinations, but only if those word combinations occur with other word combinations for which it is never the case that yet other words combinations occur with the first group.

## REINFORCEMENT LEARNING IN ARTIFICIAL MINDS

Contrary to human minds, artificial minds do not have biological behaviour. They do not salivate when computationally seeing meat as in Pavlov's studies, or express fear when hearing loud clanging noise as in Watson's experiments. Classical conditioning is hard to imagine in machines. But just like Skinner's pigeons in operant conditioning, artificial minds can be trained in operant conditioning. They too can be reinforced to perform a particular behaviour. Operant conditioning in the machine learning literature is suitably called "reinforcement learning".

Just like Skinner needed a pigeon or a rat that gets reinforced to perform a particular behaviour (or avoid such behaviour), machine learning needs such an agent. An agent that learns to make decisions by interacting with its environment. An agent that receives feedback in the form of rewards or penalties. The agent's goal is to learn a strategy that maximizes the reward over time, the computational version of bird food (or shocks). The machine learning agent in our example is not a pigeon, but an email detection system.

The email detection system again aims to learn to automatically filter incoming messages into two categories; the genuine and spam categories. The system learns to correctly classify emails by receiving feedback based on whether the classification it proposes is correct or incorrect. It receives the reinforcement and adjusts its behaviour on these computational rewards or punishments.

In an initial exploration phase the reinforcement learning algorithm makes mistakes. It randomly classifies emails to explore different strategies, and does not have any understanding of which emails are genuine or spam. It is like the pigeon who initially aimlessly hops around not knowing what would happen if a lever were to be pressed. However, just like the pigeon, the moment the email spam detection system happens to receive a reward (or punishment) after the first decision it makes, it starts identifying patterns in the features of spam and real emails. For example, it gets rewarded each time it puts the emails that contain the words "prince", "inheritance", "click" and "prize" in the spam category, and gets punished when it places these emails in the genuine category. Similarly, it gets rewarded when other emails are placed in the genuine category and punished when it places those in the genuine category. The rewards and punishments the email spam detection system gets are 1s and -1s. Over time the system starts to perform to a maximization of the points it gets. Over many interactions with the environment the system refines its policy and has learned which features are indicative of genuine or spam emails.

In all fairness, an email detection system is not the best example of reinforcement learning, but one consistent with the examples given for supervised and unsupervised learning. A better example of reinforcement learning is a self-driving car that needs to get to a certain target. While it is zooming in where it needs to drive to, it continuously gets rewards ("you scored a point! Great job, go there!")

or punishments ("you have just been deducted a point, don't go there!"). Over time the system learns how to navigate towards its target by continuously been rewarded or punished a bit and nudged in the right direction.

If supervised, unsupervised, and reinforcement learning need to be summarized, one could say that for supervised learning both input and output are known. The data is labelled, and what the system needs to do is learn a mathematical function that maps the labelled input to labelled output. The system learns from examples of correct outcomes. In unsupervised learning the input is known, but unlabelled. We know what data we are sending through the machine learning algorithm, but we do not know what the output will be. The machine learning algorithm discovers hidden patterns in the data with no explicit guidance. Finally, in reinforcement learning the input data is unknown. The system interacts with the environment. After going through an exploration phase, the machine learning algorithm gets rewarded or punished. The system learns by trial and error, and optimizes its behaviour based on cumulative reward.

## HOW DO HUMAN ARTIFICIAL MINDS AND HUMAN MINDS ESTIMATE ACCURACY?

Let's go back to our supervised machine learning example. Remember, our machine learning algorithm correctly identified 80% of the emails as genuine and spam. This is well above chance, when the system would have randomly categorized an email as genuine or spam, as that would have been a 50%-coin toss. But is 80% really that good?

Imagine that the 1,000 emails we test were all genuine emails. There were no spam emails whatsoever (I am looking forward to one of those days that my mailbox is liberated from spam). With 80% performance our algorithm may have placed all emails in the genuine category, without having learned a thing. Erroneously it threw 200 emails in the spam category, despite the fact that these emails were in fact genuine. In that case, 80% accuracy is not very encouraging. To avoid this problem, the training and testing sets need to be balanced with an equal number of genuine and spam emails. However, finding such a balanced dataset of genuine and spam emails is a challenge for it fortunately is the case that there are far more genuine emails than spam emails.

But let's assume that our 1,000 emails happen to be a balanced dataset, with 50% genuine and 50% spam emails. An accuracy of 80% may seem good, but here too we need to treat performance with caution. For instance, it is more important that genuine emails are not placed in the spam category than that spam emails erroneously do get placed in the genuine category. We can live with an accidental spam email in our genuine email folder, but missing out on that very important email with the job offer, the party invitation, or that date would be bad. Really bad.

Machine learning performance distinguishes between four different categories that the system uses in its evaluation. In our spam detection performance, the system may say the email is spam, and it indeed is spam, may say the email is not spam, and it indeed is no spam. Our system may also say that an email is spam, but actually it is not, or say it is not spam, but it actually is. Only by looking at all those four performance categories, we can obtain an overall understanding of how well our spam detection system is actually doing. Beyond just looking at that 80% accuracy we obtained alone.

|  | The system predicts the email is spam | The system predicts the email is genuine |
|---|---|---|
| The email is actually spam | **True positive** "Great job, only my junk mail folder fills up with spam!" | **True negative** "Great job, my inbox only consists of genuine emails." |
| The email is actually genuine | **False positive** "Oops, there accidentally goes an important email to the spam category!" | **False negative** "Oops, my inbox is not as clean as it should have been!" |

The importance of distinguishing between these four categories becomes more apparent when we compare the way artificial minds evaluate performance with the way human minds evaluate that performance. And here psychology can learn a thing or two from artificial intelligence (still no pun intended).

If an algorithm says an email is spam, how likely is it to really be spam? To figure out the real chance that an email marked as spam is actually spam, we need to know a few things: How often is the algorithm right about spam? How often is an email spam in the first place? And how often does the program mark any email as spam, regardless of whether it's spam or not? Only by looking at how often the algorithm catches spam correctly and how often it makes mistakes, can we get a better idea of whether we can trust the system when it says an email is spam. And humans tend to be pretty bad at considering these four options.

Let's illustrate this by using a more impactful example[8]. These days there are many medical AI tests that can predict with high accuracy whether you have a disease. Imagine one such test is able to detect a rare disease that affects 1 in 1,000 people (0.1%). The medical AI test is highly accurate, so accurate that with 99% sensitivity it correctly detects those carrying the disease (the true positive). With 99% specificity it also correctly identifies those without the disease (the true negative). But no medical tests, not even the AI ones, are ever perfect. We know that 1% of people who don't have the disease will still test positive (this is the false positive). We also know that 1% of people who have the disease will test negative (this is the false negative).

You take the highly accurate test on the rare disease. The next week you are called. Your doctor brings the news that the test is positive. If you are like many, you panic. You have the rare disease. Your life is turned upside down. The test is 99% accurate, and you do the calculations: The chance of accidentally not having the disease is only 1%! Despite the fact that the emotional response is understandable, your calculations are wrong. The logical consequence you have reasoned to is not at all valid. When the test comes back positive, it could be a true positive (you actually have the disease), or a false positive (you don't have the disease, but the test says you do). Out of the 1,000 people that would do the medical test, there is 1 true positive (a person who has the disease *and* tests positive) and there are about 10 false positives (people who don't have the disease but still test positive). That means that for every 11 positive results (1 true positive + 10 false positives), only 1 person actually has the disease. So, even if you tested positive, the chances that you actually have the disease are just 1 in 11, or about 9%. I am not at all downplaying the fact that 9% is still too high for having any disease, but it is considerably lower than the devastating calculations you made when not considering the true positives, true negatives, false positives and false negatives.

Why is this important for a psychology of artificial intelligence? Well, it shows that human minds often do not think logically, a conclusion we were already able to draw in Chapter 3. Human minds *think* they reason logically, and with enough cognitive effort they *can*, but too often we rely on our gut feeling rather than on solid logic. The medical test example also shows something else that is important, what psychology can learn from artificial intelligence. Psychology aims to understand why a particular behaviour occurs. Using experiments, psychology aims to understand a phenomenon and generalizes it across situations. In artificial intelligence, and machine learning specifically, the goal is to predict the future. To create a model that can make accurate predictions on new and unseen data.

Let me illustrate with an example on AI. Human minds often judge the likelihood of an event based on how easily examples come to mind. AI-powered self-driving cars causing one accident we hear about in the news, make some of us think that AI-powered self-driving cars are dangerous. Worse, we might think all AI-driven devices must be dangerous. Psychology aims to explain why human minds make such biased decisions, for instance by conducting experiments in which participants are asked whether or not they are willing to use a self-driving car. Such an experiment is worthwhile for car manufacturers of self-driving cars, as we can learn whether participants make valid decisions after being informed about an accident (and often human minds do not make those valid decisions). But such psychology experiments always look back, in hindsight. A machine learning solution would instead investigate whether such decisions can be predicted (and therefore prevented). Using true positives, true negatives, false positives, and false negatives it can help encourage us to predict when people take an AI-powered self-driving car and when not (and when this is a valid decision and when not). Explanation is useful, but predictions are sometimes perhaps even more useful, for instance for the car manufacturers of self-driving cars.

Metaphorically speaking, psychology is great at understanding what happens under the hood of a phenomenon (sometimes at the expense of being able to predict the phenomenon in the future). Artificial intelligence is great at predicting the phenomenon in the future (sometimes at the expense of understanding the mechanisms of the phenomenon).

## HOW DO ARTIFICIAL MINDS LEARN DEEP?

When it comes to a chapter of learning, the topic of deep learning cannot be ignored[9]. Deep learning is all about artificial neural networks, introduced in the previous chapter. These networks are deeper than the 1–2 hidden layer artificial neural networks in the early days, because they include far more hidden layers, dozens or even hundreds. When artificial neural networks were going out of fashion in the 1980s, rebranding them into deep learning – allowed by more data and more computing power – made them very popular again.

Deep learning is a subfield of machine learning[10]. Deep learning is able (and needs) to handle larger and more complex datasets than traditional machine learning techniques can typically handle. The deep learning coming from the artificial brains of the 1980s was still relatively straightforward. But with the advancements in computational power, a hierarchy of hidden layers in artificial neural networks became feasible so that input data could be transformed into more abstract and composite representations. By rebranding artificial neural

networks to deep learning, artificial intelligence did not only empha-
size the physical system as much as it emphasized the learning process.

In deep learning, the artificial neural network starts by receiving input. At first, the network does not know anything and makes
random guesses; guesses based on what it knows. But after each
guess, the network gets feedback, compares its guess with the correct answer, and learns whether it made a mistake. In the learning
process, the network continually adjusts the values associated with
nodes in the network to improve itself. It tweaks the weights of the
connections between the units to improve the output. Let's break
this down further. How does an artificial neural network adjust its
weights?

Let's first return to our waterways example from the previous
chapter. The input of the pile of sand, the metaphor of our artificial
neural network was coloured liquid. The output of the neural network, what the system needed to learn, was a particular colour, for
instance cyan, purple, or grey. The width of the channels through
which the dyed liquid flows could be adjusted, letting some dyed
liquid through more or less. In terms of an artificial neural network,
these are the weights. What I did not discuss in the previous chapter
is the learning of the network. The question is how the weights –
how the channels – learn to reach the highest performance of the
network. How to best get the cyan, purple, or grey colour as output?
Imagine we have a network that has red, green, and blue as input
units. Weights determine the activation of each of these three input
units, and combine their results in two output units, let's say either
the colour combination of "light blue" or "dark blue". Those are the
only two options in the output of our network. This is an extremely
simple neural network as it has no hidden layers. In this network we
pretty much know how the model needs to learn: More green and
red in addition to blue lighten the blue, little to no red darkens the
blue. If we need to adjust the weights, we have a pretty good idea
how to.

But now take a deep learning model with hidden layers. Let's take
a model with dozens of hidden layers. When you have a continuously

changing network with so many different parameters, how do you know which weights to change to have the network perform more optimally? How would the network learn? A "back-propagating error correction" is the solution. This learning rule allows for determining which parts of the model are responsible for the success of the model and which parts needed to be adjusted. So let's assume our example of creating the colour of cyan with a neural network with a hidden layer. Backpropagation compares the prediction of the network (the predicted colour), to the actual answer (the wanted colour). Working backward through the network, the learning process adjusts the weights in the network minimizing the error for future predictions. For instance, if there is too much red for cyan, weights will bring that colour down, too little green weights for cyan output will bring it up, and too little blue for cyan output will make the weights such that there is enough blue. Through backpropagation the system ultimately learns that with 0% red, 50% green and 100% blue the colour of cyan is reached[11]. Large amounts of data get sent through the network to obtain the desired output, and backpropagation allowed to continuously adjust the weights of the connections between the units to make sure that the system learned how to reach the optimal performance[12].

The idea of the network learning through backpropagation propelled advancements in artificial neural networks. All renowned researchers in deep learning – from Geoffrey Hinton to Yann LeCunn – developed different instantiations of backpropagation. Instantiations that allowed for complex neural network architectures to learn by trial-and-error[13].

Backpropagation seemed to be a fundamental aspect of artificial minds to learn. There is, however, one major drawback to backpropagation, at least for the psychology of artificial intelligence. The solution for artificial minds has no equivalent in human minds. Contrary to the direction of backpropagation, synapses in the human brain are feedforward connections that go in only one way.

Backpropagation is perhaps the most common way for artificial neural networks to learn. But certainly not the only way. There are other common techniques, several of them that better compare to learning in the human brain. For instance, some artificial neural networks also implement the idea of Hebbian learning, where "neurons that fire together, wire together." If two units in the network are activated at the same time, the connection between them gets stronger. This kind of associative learning is often used in some forms of unsupervised learning. And just like in reinforcement learning in humans, artificial neural networks can learn through trial and error by interacting with an environment and receiving rewards or punishments depending on the actions the system takes. Reinforcement learning in deep learning is often used in game playing or robotics.

Deep learning in artificial neural networks has been described here in very easy terms not doing justice to the complexity of the field. Very different types of artificial neural networks have been developed, varying in their structure, the different types of units they use, the learning rules they apply, and by introducing different kinds of randomness in the model.

Comparing artificial neural networks with human ones is tricky, as there are many differences. But in the vein of this book, let's look at the similarities. Because of their learning capabilities, artificial neural networks, just like human ones, have become dynamic. Because of their different architectures artificial neural networks, just like the human ones, have different specializations excelling at different tasks depending on the architecture. And just like regarding human neural networks, the mechanisms of the artificial ones have become increasingly hard to understand.

# 6

## HOW DO HUMAN AND ARTIFICIAL MINDS UNDERSTAND LANGUAGE?

One of the fundamental questions in both cognitive psychology and artificial intelligence is the question of how human and artificial minds make sense of the seemingly random characters presented on a page like this. Or the seemingly arbitrary sounds they hear when somebody talks to them, the fundamental question of how human and artificial minds understand language. The general assumption in psychology and artificial intelligence is that if we manage to answer the question regarding how language attains meaning, we also better understand the very basis of how the mind works. The human and artificial minds alike.[1]

### HOW DO HUMANS MINDS UNDERSTAND LANGUAGE?

Understanding how human minds understand language is a pre-requisite for understanding human minds. "When we study human language, we are approaching what some might call the 'human essence', the distinctive qualities of mind that are, so far as we know, unique to man."[2] These are the words of Noam Chomsky, one of the attendees of the 1956 MIT workshop that introduced the cognitive revolution, and the linguist who defined decades of language

DOI: 10.4324/9781003491095-6

research. Of course, animals too have communication systems. But they do not have a language system as we know it. And consequently, as the (albeit incorrect) inference goes, humans are more intelligent than other non-human animals. Or more broadly and equally incorrectly: only a species that really uses language can think, and if you can think you are intelligent. Animals don't have human language and can therefore not really think and are therefore not really intelligent. And what is true for non-human animal minds is true for non-human artificial minds. A rather arrogant self-fulling prophecy on our human side.

One of the central features of language is that language is arbitrary[3]. There is no specific or necessary connection between the sounds of the words we use and the message we thereby communicate. This arbitrariness principle was proposed by the French linguist Ferdinand de Saussure and has had a major impact on research on language and cognition. Think about it. We call a four-legged animal that barks a "dog". There is no intrinsic relation between the sound of the word "dog" and the meaning of that word. The same four-legged animal is called *chien* in French and *hond* in Dutch. Different sounds for the very same concept. Any concept we can think of in any language has a combination of arbitrary sounds. There are some exceptions to the principle of arbitrariness, such as "woof-woof" which refers to the sound a dog makes (and not arbitrarily to the sound a cat makes). In French or Dutch, the spelling may be somewhat different ("ouaf-ouaf", "waf-waf") but the sounds are pretty much the same. But looks (and sounds apparently) are deceiving, as the Indonesian "guk guk" and the Italian "bau bau" demonstrate. Still a dog-barking sound for those languages but with sounds arbitrary to native English speakers. Overall, however, for the vast majority of words in our dictionary, there is an arbitrary relation between the sound of a word and its meaning, as the almost 7,000 languages in the world demonstrate, languages whose lion's share of concepts are referred to by a vast repertoire of different sounds.

It seems that the arbitrariness principle in language can be extended beyond sounds. Not only are there arbitrary relations between the sound of a word and its meaning, there are also seemingly arbitrary relations in combinations of words, in the sentence structure. I can say "Max ate a sandwich" or "a sandwich Max ate" and the meaning is (pretty much) the same. Speakers of Hixkaryana, in Pará and Amazonas states of Brazil, or Urarina, spoken in Northwest Peru, would instead use the (translated) structure "a sandwich ate Max" and some 328 million Austronesian language users would prefer "ate a sandwich Max", for the exact same meaning. A meaning that would not at all involve man-devouring sandwiches. Sure, across languages some structures are more common than others, but overall, the choice of a structure seems to be arbitrary.

And arbitrariness in language can also get extended beyond sound and sentence structure. It is not only the sound of a word or the structure of a sentence that have a non-fixed meaning across languages, as language users we have even more seemingly random flexibility at our disposal in what we talk about. We can as easily talk about "pink elephants playing boomerang in the ocean" as we can talk about "green ideas sleep furiously". Seemingly arbitrary distributions of words on seemingly arbitrary topics we can seemingly randomly talk about. We presumably have full freedom in the company our words keep. We are fully liberated when it comes to our language production.

Human minds are true magicians of the symbol system we call language. With all this flexibility, learning a language for a child becomes extremely challenging, as any second-language learner appreciates. Words will have to be memorized, grammatical rules need to be learned, and all the words need to be placed in the right context. After all, the flexibility of the producer of the language should not lead to confusion in the receiver of that language. The message conveyed by the speaker should be understood correctly by the hearer. And yet within approximately two years of age, a child is able to produce its first sentences, and language comprehension takes place well before that. How does it do that?

How do human minds acquire this arbitrary symbol system called language? One answer might be that children learn language by being taught that language. Children may learn to speak by mimicking what they hear and from encouragement from their parents when they get the language right, some kind of operant conditioning discussed in the previous chapter. Parents compliment children on their language production, which encourages children to continuously improve their language skills. The problem is that children produce sentences they have never heard before, undermining the idea that they only mimic language they hear. Moreover, parents do not always provide feedback to their children and if they do, they don't always give the right feedback. A toddler producing her very first words saying "ma-ma" to daddy, will not be punished, or otherwise receive non-positive feedback about the incorrect reference, but will instead be applauded for the effort producing *anything*. And thus receive incorrect feedback. And yet children distinguish mummy from daddy, and learn to find the corresponding words. Language acquisition seems very different from a pigeon learning how to make a silhouette.

Another answer to the question how human minds acquire language is that children are born with an innate ability to acquire language. Some universal grammar system happens to be pre-wired in the newborn brain. Some kind of language acquisition device or language instinct. The view of language parameters in the brain has dominated linguistics in the last part of the 20th century, and is a common view even shared today. There is a lot to say about this view, but for now it suffices to say that this view only focuses on one aspect of language, its syntax. According to many, it is syntax, the grammatical structuring of words in a sentence that makes language, and human language processing, so special. But for the purposes of this chapter, we focus on understanding language, how to capture *meaning* more than determining grammaticality.

Undoubtedly influenced by research on the brain, both the human and artificial neural architectures, another answer may be that children learn language through neural connections. By being exposed to patterns in language, the child's brain forms connections that allow children to understand and produce language. According to this theory language learning was considered a process of building associations between sounds, words, and meanings based on repeated exposure. Unsupervised learning. Language acquisition through a neural network. Let me illustrate this theory with a quote from linguist J.R. Firth who stated, "You shall know a word by the company it keeps."[4] Firth argued that language users are able to extract the meaning of words from the contexts in which these words are used. Let me explain.

If I asked you what a plurp means, you'd probably have no idea. The word is arbitrary as the sound of the word has no relation to its meaning. Now instead of hearing the single word "plurp" you heard the sentence that "I was chased by a plurp, while walking to work this morning". Whereas you earlier had no idea of the meaning of plurp, you may now have at least some idea of what "plurp" means. An idea that is based on the company the word "plurp" keeps. "You may not know the exact meaning of the word "plurp", but you do know that it is unlikely to be a paperclip, a table, or a colour." You may safely assume it is more likely some kind of animal that is able to chase people that are walking. Not so much an extinct dinosaur or an exotic tiger, and more likely some kind of doglike or a catlike creature. Basically, you get to know the meaning of the word "plurp" by the company it keeps. It is as if language users replace the unknown word by another word in order to find the meaning of plurp. When considering "I was chased by a ____, while walking to work this morning", try "dog" or "cat" to fill in the blanks and there seems to be a match. Try "table" or "paperclip" and there is not.

But the idea that human minds know the meaning of a word by the company it keeps received a lot of backlash in the psychological sciences[5]. Philosopher John Searle illustrated the criticism by introducing a thought experiment, called the Chinese Room argument[6].: Imagine you are locked up in a room with no windows. All the room has is a mailbox flap that opens and through which a combination of symbols written on a piece of paper arrive on your desk. On the other side of the room another mailbox flap is located through which you can give your answer. That is your task: You receive a combination of symbols, let's say 你叫什么名字. On your desk you have a question-answering book that links questions to answers. You look up the symbol combination and find the corresponding answer, 不关你的事, and write down that answer and submit it through the output mailbox flap.

The fundamental question now is whether the person, by taking a Chinese question and answering that question in Chinese, actually understands the Chinese language. And the answer to that question is simple: Of course not! Language comprehension is more than translating symbols into other symbols into other symbols. Language comprehension is more than a symbolic merry-go-round[7] translating one word into another, more than "knowing" a word through other words it keeps company.

Based on the idea that linguistic symbols have arbitrary relations to their meaning, embodied cognition researchers argued that for language to become meaningful it is essential that words are grounded in the environment or perceptual experiences. Symbol grounding is critical for understanding language. A "plurp" does not become meaningful because of other words that can substitute the word "plurp". Because of all the arbitrariness in language it simply cannot! Instead, "plurp" becomes meaningful by having seen a plurp in the world around us, in our visual memory or our visual imagination. By having heard a plurp, touched a plurp, smelled a plurp – or admittedly depending on the meaning of the word – tasted a plurp. Language comprehension is fundamentally embodied, just like cognition is embodied. Human minds are embodied. Who we are, what we do, how we behave, cannot be seen isolated from our bodies and the environment we move around in. The argument the Chinese Room argument put forward (and embodied cognition researchers strongly advocated), is one catastrophic for artificial intelligence, because AI does exactly that: translating symbols into other symbols. At best computers would be able to show similarities in their performance with humans, following the embodiment logic they can never understand language! With computers not having visual, auditory, olfactory, gustatory and tactile senses they would miserably lose out on understanding language. According to this argument at least.

## HOW DO ARTIFICIAL MINDS UNDERSTAND LANGUAGE?

Criticism on the symbol-merry-go-round folly particularly came from the field of psychology. After all, psychology researchers argued that if the person in the Chinese Room is not able to understand language, we must conclude AI would never be able to understand language, for this is exactly what artificial minds do. Artificial minds translate an arbitrary symbol combination such as 0111001110101 into another arbitrary symbol combination 110110011. And if cognition is fundamentally embodied, the consequences for artificial minds would be severe, not only for natural language processing, but also for artificial neural networks for any human cognitive task imaginable. Embodied cognition researchers argued that AI never explained what was going on in their models (but forgot to add that they never built such models themselves and attempted to predict).

Despite the criticism from psychology, and the experimental evidence in favour of embodied cognition, artificial intelligence moved on, and built solutions that mimicked human language understanding (and conveniently ignored whether the machine would truly understand language the way humans do). The following conversation between me and my therapist I recently recorded.

therapist: Is something troubling you?
me: I wonder about the relation between human and artificial minds in language understanding.
therapist: That's quite interesting.
me: Thank you. The question that keeps me wondering is what the relationship between human and artificial minds is.
therapist: What are your feelings now?

me:        Well, I am interested and curious in hopes of finding an answer.

therapist: How long have you been interested and curious in hopes of finding an answer?

me:        Basically, since I started writing this chapter, but actually throughout my research career.

The name of my therapist is "Eliza", named after Eliza Doolittle, the main character in George Bernard Shaw's play Pygmalion (1913) and its musical adaptation, *My Fair Lady* in 1956 (that famous year again). Eliza asks Professor Higgins for elocution lessons, how to speak and behave properly according to the etiquette of the elite London society. And in both speech and manners Eliza does well. Except that Eliza is not human, but artificial (and not my therapist). ELIZA was the first chatbot that seemed intelligent, as one could have natural conversations with the computer. Developed by MIT computer science professor Joseph Weizenbaum, ELIZA showed two things in particular. One was that humans are very willing to anthropomorphize computers[8]. In the example above, it is odd for me thanking a computer for its input. But I bet you have done the same when talking to a chatbot. Secondly, with some very simple rules the impression is created that we can have a meaningful conversation with a computer. ELIZA looks very intelligent. By just taking a snippet from the user input, and putting that snippet together with some general rules "why do you think that?" (for a statement and not a question), "why do you think that [snippet]", "how long have you been interested in [snippet]", the algorithm can keep the conversation going on for a while. And for those readers who would argue "but that seems a rather shallow conversation!", I invite you to analyse the small talk many of us are familiar with in the hallway of our offices or that party in the weekend. Occasions where we apply simple rules without going into depth regarding the meaning of the utterance. "How are you?", "I am fine, thank you!"; "you look wonderful tonight!", "How's your family doing?" Often human conversation is shallow, and the first natural language processing (NLP) robot ELIZA took advantage of it.

No matter how impressive ELIZA was (and still is), the problem is that it really (but really!) does not "know" anything. It keeps the conversation going in a seemingly meaningful way, and uses rules conveniently, but it does not compute any meaning. If the user states "I feel bad", ELIZA responds "why do you feel bad?" For "good", "disgusted", or "plurpy", it will respond in exactly the same way ("why do you feel ____?"). Now, small talk at an average party might indeed not exceed the mechanisms ELIZA employs, but one would hope that your conversational partner would pick up on "disgusted" or "plurpy".

Models that aim to compute the semantics of language, its meaning, and claim to actually 'understand' language, often use distributional semantics or word embeddings. Just like artificial neural networks had the advantage of parallel distributed processing solving the problems Symbolic AI was struggling with, distributional semantics solved those problems, specifically rigidity and scalability problems[9]. Distributional semantics worked off Firth's idea that we know the meaning of a word by the company it keeps. A distributional semantics model computes the likelihood words (or sentences of paragraphs or texts) appear together. Let's consider the sentence "the dog chases the cat". One could argue that the meaning of the word "dog" and the word "cat" must have some meaning in common simply because the two words appear in the same sentence, in Firth's words: keep each other company. But such a conclusion requires that we have a sentence somewhere in our training set that includes both words. If such a sentence is lacking, "dog" and "cat" presumably have nothing in common. Imagine that the dataset we use indeed lacks that sentence, but does include the sentence "a man owns a dog" and "the woman owns the cat". The fact that there are two sentences that both include the word "own", indirectly "dog" and "cat" do have some meaning in common (through "own") at a higher level. And we can extend this further. No sentence with "dog" and "cat" at a first-order level, the sentences "a man owns a dog" and "the woman has the cat" at the second-order level, may still distribute meaning about "dog" and "cat" at the third-order level through a sentence like "both the man and the woman have a pet" – and in this distributed process, meanwhile, construct the meaning that "dog" and "cat" likely are "pet".

More technically, what distributional semantics does is take in a large body of text – 10 million words or so in tens of thousands of paragraphs. It then creates an imaginary spreadsheet of terms (words) and documents (paragraphs) and computes the frequency with which a word appears in each of these paragraphs. In paragraphs on politics the words "party", "minister" and "government" have frequencies higher than 0. In paragraphs on pets, the words "party", "minister" and "government" have zero frequencies, but "dog" and "cat" have higher frequencies. This massive matrix is rather sparse. It mostly consists of zeros (because few paragraphs are about politics and pets and all other topics in the language dataset. This massive term x document matrix is then summarized using matrix algebra, so that the frequencies in each cell of the matrix become summaries of those frequencies. And then the magic starts. The meaning of a word becomes a vector, a dimension in space, a word embedding. Even though artificial minds can think in countless dimensions, human minds can only think in three dimensions, four at best if you include time. Talking about intelligence! In a simplified three-dimensional solution, the word "dog" points in one direction based on all the words it keeps company, and the word "cat" points in a similar (but not the same) direction because of the same reason. The word "government" points in a very different dimension. A distributional semantic model however can easily deal with 300 dimensions! The word "dog" may now have become a 300-dimensional vector in space!

Simple mathematics can compute the distances between vectors. If a word vector points in a similar dimension as another word vector, their relation gets a higher value than the relation with a word that points in a different direction. These word embedding models demonstrated to be very powerful, as they allow for computing the

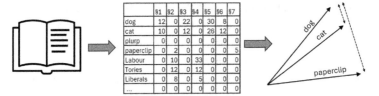

**Figure 6.1** Distributional semantics: from text to matrix to word vectors

semantic similarity probability between two words. They estimate the meaning between words. "Dog" and "cat" would have a semantic similarity score of .9, whereas "dog" and "government" yields a score of .1. The latter two could potentially appear in language, but hardly ever do, and if they do certainly with a lower probability than "dog" and "cat".

But what can be done for words, can also be done for sentences, for paragraphs, and for texts. Using distributional semantics, the semantic similarity between linguistic units larger than words could be computed. Suddenly automated question answering systems became feasible. A question such as "What is the relation between human and artificial minds in language understanding" could be answered by finding the sentence with the highest semantic similarity score between the question-sentence and a potential answer-sentence. The exact structure of the sentence did not matter. "I wonder about language understanding, and the relation between artificial minds and human minds" would result in selecting the same answer-sentence.

The success of distributional semantics was shown by having these models pass tests developed for human minds. For instance, implementations of these models managed to get a passing grade in the Scholastic Aptitude Test (SAT), a standardized exam used for college admissions in the US, and the Test of English as a Foreign Language (TOEFL) test, used to evaluate the English language skills of foreign students. The AI argument was that if these artificial minds managed to pass a test that human minds can, these artificial minds must be like human minds. Pretty much akin to the argument posed by Alan Turing in the Turing test.

With increasing evidence that these models matched human performance, the excitement about distributional semantic models, also called word embedding models, grew. But the criticism from psychology that these models were only able to explain performance post-hoc, combined with the AI Effect, where accomplishments by AI models were downplayed because they had not quite reached the next frontier, led to disappointment. Sure, these models managed to uncover hidden relationships between words and documents and create word embeddings to capture semantic similarity. But they could not *generate* text! Language understanding was one thing, language generation another. Generative AI was seen as the real frontier of intelligence.

## HOW DO ARTIFICIAL MINDS GENERATE LANGUAGE?

On 30 November 2022 AI became truly intelligent. No, *really* this time! In the 1950s it had become intelligent with General Problem Solving, but in the 1960s it had *really* become intelligent with the first artificial neural networks. In the 1990s it had really, *really* become intelligent with the first chess computer beating a chess champion. In the 2010s AI had become actually intelligent with AlphaGo beating a Go champion. But in 2022 AI had become actually *really* intelligent. AI had reached its next frontier by releasing Generative AI. On that day ChatGPT was released. The user could type in a simple question or statement, and within a split second you could see ChatGPT type an answer back to you. A search engine like Google would find a document that is closest to the question of what the meaning of life is. It would for instance find a document called "The meaning of life", or "The true meaning of life" or "Five simple ways to determine the meaning of life." ChatGPT did not find a document. It did not even find an existing text. Instead, it generated an answer on the fly from scratch. An answer that may not (or may) exist anywhere! ChatGPT did not look up the question and find a piece of text that provides the answer to the question. It *understood* the question and *created* the answer. In 2022 its performance was mind blowing.

However, as with all the other breakthroughs in AI, the AI Effect was the fly in the ointment. Sure, ChatGPT was impressive, but in hindsight it was not really, some started to argue. The Internet soon flooded with examples where ChatGPT was not able to count correctly. It was giving incorrect information. It was even making things up. At times ChatGPT appeared to be hallucinating! Each example of what ChatGPT was unable to do was evidence of the AI Effect: once an algorithm had reached the finish line of intelligence, us smart humans moved the finish line to be able to conclude that the original findings were really not that impressive. But the accomplishments *were* that impressive, certainly considering where artificial minds came from. Moreover, what standard did we hold ChatGPT up to? A human standard? In that case ChatGPT was able to outsmart us easily. Ask ChatGPT to write a limerick on pink elephants in London and you'll get the answer in a few seconds. Ask that question to your friend, and you may never get an answer (and lose a friendship).

Distributional semantics, word embedding, is complex. In the case of language understanding inherently unstructured language data needs to be converted into structured data. Texts need to be broken down into words and paragraphs and an imaginary structured spreadsheet marks the frequencies with which words appear in the paragraphs, and ultimately places words in a somewhat structured multidimensional space. But language generation is far more complex, as it swaps the direction from unstructured to structured. It takes in structured data – for instance the words in a multidimensional space – and must generate unstructured data, which we recognize as language. To make the difference between Natural Language Understanding and Natural Language Generation more concrete, let's use an analogy in Sudoku. Language understanding is like solving a Sudoku puzzle, where you take unstructured data, and extract 'meaning' to complete the structure. Language generation on the other hand is like creating a Sudoku puzzle, where you generate new unstructured data from structured data. If you did master solving a Sudoku puzzle, you probably have not mastered creating a Sudoku puzzle. When a computer understands language, it does not generate language. Meanwhile, to generate language it is worthwhile understanding language.

These days most of us are very familiar with ChatGPT, Claude, Copilot, DeepSeek, Gemini, Llama, or Mistral. Almost on a daily basis additional applications come out that are built on the very idea that OpenAI demonstrated in November 2022. So let's stick with ChatGPT for illustrative purposes. Just like distributional semantic models, ChatGPT is based on a Large Language Model, an LLM. The language models used in common distributional semantic models varied between 100 Megabytes to 3–5 Gigabytes. They were pretty large. If we assume that an average page of text holds about 2,000 characters and each character occupies about 1 byte of storage space, then the number of pages to train these distributional semantic models varies between 50,000 to 2,500,000 pages of text. In comparison ChatGPT4 was trained on 26 billion pages of text! Hard to grasp? That is almost 1.5 million years of newspapers. Or three times all the pages present in the British Library in London. When it is stated that ChatGPT uses Large Language Models, those models really deserve their name.

All those large language data need to be trained. In the case of ChatGPT a transformer architecture is used for training, a deep learning architecture that knows how to deal with sequences of data. When you put large amounts of training data into these transformer models, the model breaks down the data into smaller parts, say words[10]. That must sound familiar after the explanation of how distributional semantics works. The key feature of a transformer is its ability to understand context (Firth's "knowing the word by the company it keeps"). Transformer models use an attention mechanism for the model to focus on different parts of the input text to understand the relationships between words. To understand the context of each word by considering the relation to every other word. And just like the training data in ChatGPT is so much larger than the training data for distributional semantic models, so is the computational power needed to train these data. Power consumption to train a distributional semantics model before 2022 would be hundreds to thousands of watts, power consumption to train ChatGPT thousands of times that number over weeks or months!

Impressive numbers perhaps, but how do these LLMs work? The answer is basically "like an artificial neural network." A massive network with massive amounts of language training data flowing through the network. Where a question as input leads to an extensive answer as output because of the many channels and the massive amount of training materials. Explaining it in detail would be difficult. First of all, because much of the information regarding what algorithms have been used remains behind tightly closed company doors. OpenAI apparently is not that open, and the same is true for any other company releasing these chatbots. When money talks, doors close. And second, the complexity of the model is such that an easy explanation is hardly feasible. Explaining a simple artificial neural network with one hidden layer was hard, one with 256 layers and attention mechanisms forms a major challenge. This is exactly the problem with many massive artificial neural network architectures: they become unexplainable.

But you are reading this book to understand artificial minds, so here we go. Large Language Models (LLMs) master combining what linguists have called a selection axis and a combination axis. Consider a large spreadsheet where the columns are the selection axis, the semantics, and the rows the combination axis, the syntax. The columns look at the selection of words, the rows at the combination of words. However, different than in spreadsheets, we can move the columns upward and downward, and the rows leftward and rightward. Pretty much a moving chess board. Imagine you ask your favourite LLM "what is the capital of France?" This sentence is placed on a row of the spreadsheet. ChatGPT breaks down each word of the sentence and puts it in a cell. Now each of the columns of the spreadsheet can move up and down. And each of the words in each column relate to a word that is entered. The column with the cell "what" has words like "who", "why", and "where". The column with "is" has the words "are", "was", and "were". The columns with "capital" has "city", "town", "location". And finally the cell with "France" has "country",

"United Kingdom", "Europe". Basically, the columns have distributional semantic information that matches a given word to all the words that are similar in meaning. Based on moving the columns up and down the LLM thus 'knows' that a question is asked ("what") and that we are looking for a city in the country of France. Just by knowing a word by the company it keeps. But the LLM can also move its rows. In the rows of the spreadsheet the cells before and after the word that is listed does not so much give the word similar in *meaning*, but the most likely word in a *sequence*, the most likely previous word and the most likely next word in the language it has been trained on. "What" is followed by "is", "capital" is preceded by "the" and followed by "of", the word "France" is preceded by "in" and followed by "is". Our input "what is the capital of France?" allows for the LLM to generate "the capital of France is" simply by moving the row rightward. It could even generate "a city in a country in Europe is". And by using distributional semantics, we can obtain that "Paris" is the closest semantic match for the capital of France.

The illustrations are an embarrassing over-simplification of the way Large Language Models work. ChatGPT, Claude, Copilot, DeepSeek, Gemini, Llama, Mistral, or what have you. But it gives a general picture. Now imagine that the two-dimensional spreadsheet here is not two-dimensional but multidimensional. Imagine that in a three-dimensional spreadsheet there are columns that do not give the word most similar in meaning, but the word that sounds most similar. In the column of "France" the words "chance", "stance" and "dance" are listed. In the columns of "is" the word "kiss", "miss", "this". And with this extra dimension we can create different semantic constructions, syntactic constructions and even rhyming constructions. LLMs can now work like a game of charade[11] on steroids. As you know, in a game of charades one player acts out a given word or phrase to an audience, where the audience need to guess what the player intends to say. In the case of LLMs let's say the player does not act out a word or phrase, but a sentence or text. LLM is the audience and wonders "what is the next word?", "what is another word for this word", "how can we put these pieces together?" Let's give it a try: "Other word for rug in front of your door"; "The cat sat on the ____?" "Something you wipe your feet on"; "three-letter word that rhymes with "hat". In hundreds of dimensions.

It is easy to downplay the performance of LLMs by claiming all they do is predicting the next word in a sentence. They only move around the columns and rows a bit and predict what comes next. Now *that* would be an over-simplification. After all, predicting the next word requires understanding the previous words, just as with human minds. Almost 70 years after Firth's adage "you shall know the word by the company it keeps" we say, "you shall know the meaning of word by the semantic company it keeps", "you shall know the syntactic meaning of word by the syntactic company it keeps", and "you shall know the rhyme of word by the rhymes it keeps" in a tens of thousands multidimensional space whereby attention mechanisms zoom in what corners of the LLM space to pay attention to.

Large Language Models are powerful, but not seldomly they suffer from hallucinations. Ask "who authored the book *Understanding Artificial Minds through Human Minds: The Psychology of Artificial Intelligence*", and the answer ChatGPT4 gives is that "*Understanding Artificial Minds through Human Minds: The Psychology of Artificial Intelligence* was written by Geoffrey Hinton and Joscha Bach." The subsequent question "What books did Geoffrey Hinton and Joscha Bach co-author?" yields the answer "Geoffrey Hinton and Joscha Bach have not co-authored any books." Why do these models hallucinate? Given the above description, the answer should be clearer. First, the quality of the information the LLM is trained on is important. "Garbage in, garbage out" still applies; also for LLMs – even though the neural network is able to filter out many errors and inconsistencies. Secondly, the LLMs generate their answers based on the most likely words that are semantically related or are likely to follow. Even though Hinton and Bach never co-authored, 2024 Nobel prize winner Hinton is a pioneer in the field of neural networks and deep learning, Bach is known for his work on cognitive architectures, consciousness, and the philosophy of AI. They are both common names in the field of AI. LLMs readily go for the common (because frequent) answers.

Finally, LLMs hallucinate because of a lack of context, or the presumed wrong context. In the example above the assumption that is provided by the user is that there is a published book "*Understanding Artificial Minds through Human Minds: The Psychology of Artificial Intelligence.*" The moment one provides the information that the book may not yet be, or has only recently been published, the LLM will provide the right answer ("the author might not be well known yet.").

It is ironic that these hallucinations are often magnified in the media. What these hallucinations really do is show how humanlike LLMs are. Ask at a party how many animals of each kind Moses took on his ark and you will get an answer: "Two of course!". You won't call on your conversational partner that they are hallucinating. And yet, that is exactly what we do when we see artificial intelligence make the same mistake.

## HOW DO HUMAN AND ARTIFICIAL MINDS IN PART UNDERSTAND LANGUAGE?

Large Language Models have demonstrated some wonderful achievements. They do not excel in what is called AI *precision* – how accurate the model is in providing very detailed information. Early implementations, for instance, were not able to perform very basic calculations or simple logic. If you asked to compute the number of a characters in a word or sentence, the system got confused. And a question such as "Mike's mom had three sons, Huey, Dewey, and . . .?" did not quite give the correct answer. At the same time, Large Language Models excelled at what AI calls *recall*, being complete in its answers. Some argued that given the lack of precision, these models did not excel as AI models. Ironically, human minds often do not excel in precision, but do perform well on recall. Ask me the name of that particular actor, and the exact name may not come to mind, but I am happy to keep the conversation going by talking about her – "she was in that one movie with the other actor, where she was the flight instructor."

LLMs can almost be seen as a language of thought. Except that the early LLMs only used symbols. Human minds can think of pictures, sounds, smells, tastes, touches. The early instantiations of LLMs could not. Today's LLMs have become more multimodal by combining language and image data. But when such information is entered in the models, the models have shown not to improve that much. It is as if language has encoded this perceptual information[12].

Another problem with these models is that they do not know syntax. Earlier I stated that humans have language acquisition devices with parameters for syntax. LLMs do not have such a language acquisition device and can therefore not know the difference between grammatical and ungrammatical sentences. But they do. Apparently, word order can provide us with valuable information about the grammatical structure of sentences, even if the (artificial) mind does not have a language instinct. If you are a language learning human mind, or an artificial one, continuously hearing "the plurp", "the blorp", "the smark" make you cluster in an unsupervised fashion that plurp, blorp and smark have something in common. And if you hear "the plurp" very frequently, but "the dorn plurp" and "the dorn blorp" fairly frequently you may over time form noun phrases and adjectival phrases. Grammar can be bootstrapped from training materials[13]. It may not be the full story, but according to the accomplishments of large language models at least an important part.

But wait. Wait! These LLM models only translate symbols into other symbols and therefore participate in the symbol merry-go-round! Consequently, they are stuck in the Chinese Room argument. The pivotal claim in the Chinese Room argument is that language is arbitrary. Language is like computer code, consisting of arbitrary patterns of 1's and 0's!

The claim that human language is arbitrary is hard to uphold. Of course there are clear patterns in language. As language users we may feel liberated, but we are working within constraints. The word "xtduoe" does not exist in English, and any speaker knows this after reading the first characters. And the sentence "not question that to to or be be the is" is not an English sentence. Particular sound and word patterns are allowed in a language, whereas many are not.

Recent research shows that the relation between the sound of word and its meaning is not arbitrary[14]. That research does not state the opposite, that the relation is fixed, but argues that the relation is not strictly arbitrary. The sound of a word across several languages can predict whether a word is more likely a noun or a verb. The sound of a word can tell whether a word more likely has a positive or a negative connotation in different languages. The sound of a word can predict whether the word is more related to visual, auditory or olfactory experiences.

The same is true for the order in which words are presented. We seem to have full flexibility to choose a random word order, but we do not. It is more likely that we let positive words precede negative words ("there are good days and bad days"), that we let words that are high in our perceptual world precede words that are down ("from my head down to my toes"), and that we let male words precede female words ("father and mother, brothers and sisters, aunts and uncles!"). We have full flexibility to turn the order around, but if we count how often that happens, the pattern is very clear.

If it turns out to be the case that language is not entirely arbitrary, artificial minds may be reunited with human minds. Allow me to illustrate this with a visual example. Using distributional semantics models, we could compute the semantic similarity of cities based on the way they occur in language. For instance, we could take some of the largest cities in Europe, let's say, London, Paris, Berlin, Barcelona and Madrid. We may find that the word "Madrid" and "Barcelona" are more often found in the same sentence (or rather in the same direction in the multidimensional space) than "Barcelona" and "London". If we compute the semantic similarities for these five cities, we end up with a 5 x 5 matrix of similarity distances. When we visualize these values on a 2D map we find that they correlate with

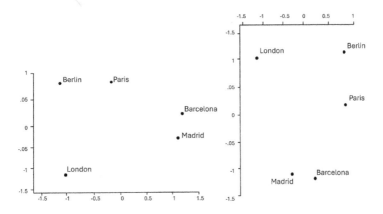

**Figure 6.2** From a symbolic merry-go-round (left) to symbol grounding (right)

the actual distances between the cities. From an AI point of view, one can argue that this is impressive as the computational model has predicted the relative locations of cities. It can create a map of Europe given that the computational estimates of the city names correlate with the location of cities (figure on the left).

However, from a psychology point of view one can argue that this does not at all represent a true geographical map. The correlations are obtained from the symbolic merry-go-round. These are not the actual longitudes and latitudes! The psychology point of view is right in that the distances on the map are relative and not absolute. But it is wrong in that the map is arbitrary. Only by grounding one of the five cities in the perceptual world, the geographical world, we can reconstruct the meaning of all five cities. We only need to know that London is the most northwestern city, or Madrid the most Southern city, and the approximate longitude and latitude of the five cities are obtained (figure on the right).

Language understanding in artificial minds may seem different than that of human minds because the artificial minds struggle with embodiment and with feelings. But perhaps they are different only by a bit. Human minds are good at creating meaning. However, given that you know the meaning of a word also by the company it keeps, language itself also creates meaning. Hidden in the language structures, the way we have used words on the selection and combination axis of our mental spreadsheet, language has encoded its meaning. Encodings ready for human and artificial minds to use.

# 7

## HOW DO HUMAN AND ARTIFICIAL MINDS PERCEIVE?

Most of what has been discussed so far covered linguistic and mathematical symbols and how AI models categorize, compute and generate their combinations. But much of the world around us is far richer than symbolic information. A picture is worth a thousand words, if not more. We make sense of the world around us because of what we perceive in that world. Sights, sounds, smells, tastes and touches taken in by a sensory system are all processed by an information processing system to give meaning to the rich sensory information around us. In both human and artificial minds.[1]

### HOW DO HUMAN MINDS SEE?

When we open our eyes, light enters through the cornea. The black hole in our eye, interestingly literally a hole, changes its size to let light into the eye. Our pupil consequently becomes smaller when bright light enters and larger when the amount of light goes down. That light then hits the back of the eye, the cornea. Some 126 million photoreceptors in the human retina respond to that light. About 120 million of them, called rods, are specialized in low light perception. These rods excel at sensing movement and shapes in dim lighting, and are good at peripheral vision. Some 6 million

DOI: 10.4324/9781003491095-7

photoreceptors, called cones, excel in higher light levels. The cones specialize in colour vision and fine detail. The output of the 126 million photoreceptors in the retina is then relayed to the brain by retinal ganglion cells. But only by 1.2 million cells. This means that the retina does not deliver to the brain a pixel-by-pixel representation of what the eyes see, but a pre-processed signal, reducing the 126 million photoreceptors to 1.5 million cells. These retinal ganglion cells extract different attributes of the image. For instance, they pluck out the spatial contrast, the colour, the motion, and deliver all this information to different areas of brain[2]. Basically, what happens when the sense organs detect a stimulus is that the sensory receptors, when they receive physical stimulation, produce a neural signal. Next a "where/how" pathway extends to the parietal regions of the brain specialized in spatial information. A "what" pathway extends to the temporal regions of the brain to identify objects.

When we look in front of us, we see light, but that light is immediately translated into stuff. One major challenge for the human brain is how to segment objects the eyes see. Psychologists in the 1930s proposed so-called Gestalt principles of organization. For instance, human minds group visual stimuli that look alike. That is a good thing when you watch your football match. The players of the team with the same colour shirt are all grouped into one team. Similarly, human minds group stimuli that are in close proximity. That is a good thing too. While you are reading the words of this page, each word is perceived as a unit of information. Letters in close proximity are grouped as one word. The sentence "therapist is now here" means something very different from "the rapist is nowhere" because of the principle of proximity. We also group items based on a principle of good continuation. The symbol ≠ could be perceived as four horizontal lines, two on the left of the slash, and two on its right. Instead, we perceive an equal sign with a slash through it. Similarly, if you look at somebody standing behind a desk, you are not horrified this person has lost her legs. Instead thanks to the principle of good continuation you assume that the body of the person you see continues even if it is visually blocked by an object, in this case a desk. And finally, we use the principle of closure. Our brain will fill in the blanks in a stimulus with missing parts to perceive a complete picture. We like coherence. We tend to view ⌒⌒ as an O, even though the symbol could be seen as a series of shapes (accidentally placed in a circle). Think of the IBM logo, the World Wildlife Fund (WWF) logo, or the Apple logo that we complete in our mind as a full uninterrupted image.

These Gestalt principles of organization help human minds to organize the physical world into objects. But how do we identify what these objects are? One answer to this question is that we apply some template matching. Human minds have stored patterns they have seen before, and with incoming information they match the shapes to the stored pattern in order to identify the object. This is probably what you are doing right now. If a character more or less looks like an /-\ it probably is an A, because of the pattern A that we carefully stored in our mind.

That makes sense for letters and numbers. Perhaps for squares and circles. We may have a template stored in our human minds, because letters, numbers, squares and circles form a finite set. But what about actual objects that consist of the combinations of several stored patterns? Take for instance the image of a giraffe. It is unlikely that we have a separate template stored in our human mind for a giraffe, another one for a zebra, another one for a horse, and yet another one for a donkey. I guess the best evidence is that if I ask you to draw one of these animals, they may look pretty much the same – depending on your drawing skills – except for their major differences. That is, drawn letters, numbers and shapes will likely look more similar than more complex objects. Researchers have argued that we recognize those objects by their components. It may not (only) be the case that we store templates in our human minds, but we also store components that make up objects. We break an object down in geometric shapes that are stored and these visual pieces of an object are ultimately configured into that object. The visual pattern of a giraffe is like a horse (and zebra and donkey), except that the giraffe has geometric subcomponents of a neck and legs that are longer than those of a horse (and zebra and donkey).

The problem with the template-matching and the recognition-by-components is that all these patterns need to be stored in memory. What if we see an object that we cannot match, or its subcomponents have not yet been determined? A very unusual object consisting of very unusual shapes never seen before. Subcomponents and templates do not really work then, and yet we can still see the object.

Perhaps next to, or instead of, prestored patterns – whether sub-components or templates – we use some kind of feature analysis when identifying objects. We see a horizontal line, a vertical line, a circle, a diagonal line, all kinds of features that when put together form an object. All these different features make up an object. Again, take out that pencil to draw a giraffe and every hand stroke is pretty much a feature. But that then leaves the question, how these features allow us to recognize an object? Perhaps through the components made up out of the features. And through those templates, made up out of components. That brings us back to square one.

These different explanations – features, geometric shapes, template – make object recognition hierarchical. From lower levels, for instance the features, we work our way up to geometric subcomponents, up to templates we try to match. The process going from the bottom to the top is called bottom-up processing. The opposite however happens at the same time. From the top of the hierarchy, we work our way down. Top-down processing matches an expected image to the data that is perceived. You can easily try this out yourself. Lie down on the grass looking up at the clouds. You see all kinds of objects floating by high up in the sky, objects that you project onto the random clouds that appear. On a rainy day you can try this out too with a piece of burned toast. Again, miraculously objects appear on the piece of toast. If we do not expect an object, we typically do not see it in the clouds or the toast. Had a strictly bottom-up process been at play, we would see all kinds of random shapes in the clouds (or burned crumps). Similarly, a strictly bottom-up process would detect any small change in the environment. But we typically do not see these small differences, as you know if you've ever tried to solve a spot-the-differences puzzle.

## HOW DO ARTIFICIAL MINDS SEE?

The overview of how the human eye perceives objects – from pupil to photoreceptors to ganglion cells, from features to components to template – is important as it helps to gain insight into the question of how artificial minds recognize images. First, I should rephrase the question a bit as to how artificial minds see. The question is not so much "how do artificial minds *perceive?*" but how they *recognize*.

Image recognition or computer vision has been a complex topic in AI. One of the reasons is that in language, constraints are in place of what is, and what is not allowed. In image recognition these constraints are far less clear. In language, we know what a letter is (there are 26 in the English alphabet), and what letter combinations in a language are allowed for a word (80% of the words being 2 to 7 letters long). Sure, we can say that the equivalent of a letter or sound is a pixel, the smallest element in a computer image. But there the similarity pretty much ends. First, pixels do not appear in sequences from left to right (but also from right to left) and not only in horizontal but also in vertical order. Whereas with letters and sounds certain combination are simply not possible in a language ("xtrzyuia" comes to mind), almost any pixel combination seems possible. However, as with words, it is also true that meaningful pixel combinations that form an object consist of a configuration all possible combinations.

With few constraints on the configuration of pixels, how do artificial minds recognize images? Just like the human eye, the artificial eye starts out with light, in the form of coloured pixels. Or more precisely, it starts out with bitmaps, maps of the most basic unit of information in computers called binary digits or bits. The computerized version of an image is a bitmap formed from rows of different coloured pixels.

The idea of image recognition is that the image of pixels is investigated focus by focus. A metaphor may again be useful here. Consider image recognition by artificial minds as somebody with a microscope looking at the image. The viewer, or rather *recognizer*, investigates each part of the image slowly moving from left to right, from top to bottom. The task of the microscope viewer/recognizer is to extract features from the part of the image it sees at that time. For example, a feature might consist of highlighted areas where there are strong changes in brightness to identify the borders of objects within an image. To extract these features, filters are used, so-called kernels. Filters act like small windows that slide over the image, focusing on local regions of the image at a time. The kernels are ways for the microscope to have elements of the picture stand out. That is, the microscope can have a blurring filter, a sharpening filter, an embossing filter, or an edge detection filter. By applying each of these filters and moving along the image with the microscope, specific features of the image get emphasized. As if the microscope user makes a different-ways-to-recognize-an-object spreadsheet. The microscope user marks "I detect an edge here, check, not here, uncheck. Now let's move the microscope a bit to the right. I detect an edge here, check, and another one here, check." Then using another kernel the user marks "I detect a square here, another one here." By going through the picture with each filter, a series of feature maps emerges with each map highlighting a specific pattern.

These features maps are a series of spreadsheet matrices with the marked information of every window in the image the microscope covered. A combination of these feature maps gives a summary of the peculiarities of the images: The summary of the image broken down by its most distinct features. Once these feature maps are in place, rule-based systems can now apply template matching. The system measures how similar the features of a template are to different features of the target image. For instance, optical character recognition, whereby letters or numbers – for instance those in ancient handwritten texts – can link the perceived characters to the most likely match. And there you have it: Image recognition completed.

For a closed set of letters and numbers rule-based systems often work fine, but they struggle with more complex recognition problems. When the light changes or backgrounds are present in the image, the very specific rules and templates miss the flexibility to generalize to new images. Deep learning and artificial neural networks offer a solution. These days Convolutional Neural Networks (CNNs) are the preferred method for image recognition. These models learn patterns from data without any predefined rules. The idea is pretty much the same: a microscope scans the image to extract features from images. This is the *convolution*. Each layer in the neural network applies a set of filters to the input image. The resulting feature map highlights specific aspects of the image. The summarization of the image while keeping the most important parts is called pooling. After the filtering and scanning process (the convolution) we end up with a feature map. After several convolutional layers in the network, the extracted features are passed through fully connected layers that interpret the high-level features and classify the image into different categories. For example, in a model trained to recognize animals, the fully connected layers might classify an input image as "duck", "goose," or "cat" based on the features extracted in previous layers. When the different layers of the CNN are considered, the first layers give more of the feature information of the image – the horizontal, vertical, and diagonal lines for instance. Later layers inhibit the shapes that can be found in the image. The kernels in deeper layers learn more complex patterns such as the shapes of the objects themselves. These kernels themselves are not predefined, but are learned from the data during the training process. This all sounds complex, and image recognition is complex, but when keeping the microscope metaphor in mind, the steps made by these Convolutional Neural Networks make sense.

CNNs are artificial neural networks, and can hence learn. By adjusting the values in the filters. At the start of the training process,

**Figure 7.1** Steps in Convolutional Neural Networks in image recognition.

the filters have random values initialized randomly. But when the network gets trained on labelled data – supervised learning – the values in the filters are adjusted. The difference between the predicted image and the actual image are determined, and the network determines how much each value in a filter needs to change to reduce the difference. This is done repeatedly, until the network has learned filters that effectively capture important features in the images. Consequently, the network can adapt to different types of input data and learn to detect the most meaningful features on their own.

When comparing the processing of images in human and artificial minds, there are some illuminating similarities. The many rods and cones in our eyes gather information at a very high level, just like the pixels in an image. That information gets summarized by the retinal ganglion cells, just like the convolutional and pooling process in CNNs. The information processing part in the human perception process makes use of feature analyses, recognition-by-components and by template-matching just like the different feature maps created in the layers of the CNN. Moreover, the similarity between the human and artificial minds is that a bottom-up process in the human eye captures the visual information just like the convolution in the CNN, while a top-down process with pre-stored knowledge in the brain is applied to the incoming information just like the backpropagation process in the learning of the CNN.

Next to the illuminating similarities, there are also illuminating differences between image processing in human and artificial minds. Because CNNs are carefully looking through an image, pixel by pixel, yielding feature maps layer by layer, they can detect peculiarities in images that the human eye cannot or does not want to see. As humans, we are not easily distracted by something that blocks your view – whether it is fog, a watery eye, or an object (the Gestalt principle of good continuation discussed earlier). CNNs are far less tolerant, but the advantage is that they excel at detecting minute little changes in an image. The advantage of that "skill" is that CNNs have been very successful at scanning medical images, for instance when detecting tumours. They miss the context, which can be provided by doctors, but they can indicate when detecting something a skilled human should pay more attention to. CNNs have often shown to outperform humans in the detection of certain skin cancers, reaching a whopping performance of 95% accuracy.[3]

## HOW DO ARTIFICIAL MINDS IMAGINE?

Seeing an object, and recognizing whether its subcomponents and templates are similar to that of another object is one thing. But human minds do not simply compare one object with another. Instead, they give meaning to an object. Sure, it is worthwhile to measure the extent to which a picture of a duck is similar to the picture of a goose. And it is even more worthwhile to measure the extent to which a spot on a medical image is cancerous. But recognizing a duck or a goose from any image makes the system really smart. Having decomposed the image in different layers and having named an image as a "duck" or "goose" helps in the learning process. Imagine a large number of images of a duck as well as a large number of goose images entering the deep learning model, and by using supervised learning the network learns the features of a duck that distinguish it from a goose (e.g., a goose is larger, has a longer neck). And it learns the similarities (e.g., they both have a beak, they both have wings, they both share features).

For quite a long time, reliable image recognition formed a major frontier in computer vision. But with more images, and more labelled images, image recognition improved. Think about it, globally our online activities capture some 61,400 images *per second*. Yes, per second. Often these images are accompanied by useful captions to train an AI model, but with improved image recognition, the model can learn captions entirely by itself. If the model can determine that there is a strong similarity between one image of a duck and another image of a duck, and only the first one is labelled, it can automatically label the second one. And if there is a layer in the neural network that captures the colour of all ducks the deep learning model has seen, the model "knows" that ducks can be white, grey, brown and – given the similarities in shape with a rubber ducky – yellow.

Of course, the opposite is also true. If the network has learned what makes an image a duck, I can ask the network to retrieve an image of a duck. If the model has primarily been trained on pictures of yellow rubber duckies, it is likely that if we request an image of a duck, the model return one that is yellow. This is the reason that when entering the word "apple" in my favourite search engine, it is not the fruit that shows up, but the Apple logo. It is more likely that pictures of the popular brand are uploaded than pictures of the fruit. Similarly, it is more likely we online talk about the computer more than about the fruit. And so it goes: pictures that are more common to enter the AI models, and word meanings that are more common to enter the AI models both augment each other. LLMs and image recognition are trained on what they see most in their input data. The training material represents society. And that can also have undesirable consequences. Enter "business" and pictures of suited men show up. Enter "nurse" and pictures of female nurses show up, dressed in scrubs, the American type of scrubs because they are more frequent.

So if artificial minds can label images and can retrieve images from labels, can they also take it up a notch and *generate* images? Can they create images they have never seen before? If you have used applications such as Dall-E, Midjourney, Gemini, Firefly or any image generation application of your choice, you know the answer to this question. They can, and can do it increasingly well. The way these models work is by breaking down an image in the smallest components. Pretty much like image recognition. But they do it in an odd way. They first destruct the image. What was once a nice undamaged image, these models destroy. And once they have destructed the image, these models reconstruct it again. In the destruction phase, the AI model spreads noise over the image, blurring it until it is one big pattern of noise. What was once a wonderful image, has now gradually become a pattern of visual white noise. In the reconstruction phase the model learns how from the blurry mess of random dots the original image can be constructed again. That process does not sound very efficient, but in fact turns out to be very clever. Because in the destruction phase the model has learned what happens when you add noise, it now knows in the reconstruction phase what happens when it removes the noise. For instances, by removing certain bits of noise, shapes and colours emerge again. By removing other noise, objects emerge again, ultimately forming the clear image, and possibly a different image.

Let's break this down a bit further. If I trained a model on numerous images of a duck, and the model knows that these images represent a duck, the model – a CNN – also knows all the various visual component that make up a duck. Using LLMs the model also knows that a duck is similar to a goose. After all, you know the meaning of a word by the company it keeps as we have seen in the previous chapter. Similarly, it also knows that a duck is a bird, that it swims in water, and if the image shows any similarities to the image in a video with sound, the model could even learn that ducks make peculiar sounds (let's label that sound as quacking).

Similarly, a layer in a model trained on fire trucks may have a layer that stores the colour red. A layer in a model trained on children walking in the rain may have a layer that represents rubber boots. And series of layers trained on paintings by Van Gogh house all the ingredients that make an image Van Gogh-like. Conversely, I can now ask an image generation model to create an image of a duck in red boots in the style of Van Gogh. In image recognition that would fail because there presumably is no image of a Van Gogh style duck in red rubber boots. But in Generative AI that prompt will generate a picture out of nothing. The requested image gets created from all the abstract information stored in the many different layers forming a picture that nobody has ever seen before.

That all sounds exciting. But one critical question remains in image generation. When it comes to existing information and supervised learning, we know whether the model gets things right or wrong. The model can be trained on duck images. If the model labels an image as a goose, or worse an elephant, backpropagation can correct the weights in the model to avoid a similar mistake next time. With generated pictures we do not have labelled answers that tell the model whether it is correct or not. But here artificial minds are pretty smart again. They can measure whether the generated picture is similar to other existing component-pictures. The image of a Van Gogh-style ducky in red rubber boots must show similarities with images of Van Gogh, with images of ducks, and with images of red rubber boots. And with the abundance of digital images that comparison becomes easier to make.

But there is another trick AI has up its sleeves to test its own performance. Neural networks can compete with each other to determine how realistic a generated image is. Meet the judges Discriminator and Generator, two artificial neural networks that are part of a larger network, called a General Adversarial Network (GAN). Judge Generator generates an image from noise. Judge Discriminator is quite ready to determine whether the image is real or fake. It has been trained on numerous real images. The generated image enters the network, and the Discriminator immediately recognizes it is a fake. It tells the Generator it is a fake, or rather, it adjusts the weights in the Generator to do a better job. In this iterative process Discriminator and Generator battle things out, until the most realistic image emerges from the artificial mind of the network. And these images will become more and more realistic over time.

If we can recognize images, can classify images and can even generate images, why stop there? Why not take this a step further? What makes AI really (but really) smart is not when it can recognize images. Not even when it can generate images. But when it can recognize and generate moving images. When it can generate videos. With collections of images, videos, and audio clips, deep learning models can learn patterns in the image, video and audio data. And can generate new video frames based on learned patterns. Indeed, impossible to have imagined several years ago. And with the current applications out there – Runway, Synthesia, Pictory, Lumen5? Been there, seen that, done that.

## HOW DO HUMAN AND ARTIFICIAL MINDS RECOGNIZE FACES?

Features, shapes, geometric components, templates. So far similarities between human and artificial minds have been highlighted. And yet when it comes to visual perception, the human and artificial mind actually differ in several important respects. Human minds are fast and intuitive, can learn in an unsupervised manner with untrained data, and are not as hierarchical and segmented as CNNs are. One specific area where the differences between human and artificial minds become particularly clear is when recognizing the human face.

When humans are born, they have a strong preference for facelike patterns. So much so that it seems that human minds have innate structures of human faces[4]. Within hours of birth, the gaze of newborns is already drawn to faces, and there is evidence from brain imaging that six days after birth the baby brain is already hardwired for face recognition[5]. But our attraction to the human face is not limited to an early age. At a later age human faces still fascinate human minds. So much so that we can recall a staggering 5,000 faces[6]. And not only is our memory for faces outstanding, also the speed with which we recognize a human face is astonishing. Within 200 milliseconds the human mind can detect whether a face is familiar or not, as fast as you recognize a single word on this page[7].

It is easy to conclude that perhaps when it comes to the human face, the human brain operates at the same high precision levels as CNNs. But this does not turn out to be the case. Apparently, something else is going on. The evidence comes from manipulating images of a human face. For instance, when an image of a human face is turned 90 degrees or flipped vertically, we have a much harder time identifying the image. Similarly, we find it easier to recognize a part of a human face when it is presented within the whole face than when the part is presented in isolation. This effect is not found in images of objects. For CNNs, on the other hand, rotated images, isolated parts, faces or objects, are all the same.

Perhaps the most convincing argument that demonstrates the difference between human and artificial minds when it comes to face perception, lies in a phenomenon where features of the face – eyes and mouth – are placed reversely in an image[8]. When the image is shown in an upside-down image of the face people generally do not detect the reversed features. But when the same image is shown upright, the reverse features really (and eerily) stand out. Not only humans experience this effect, rhesus monkeys and chimpanzees have also demonstrated it[9].

There is one intelligent species for which the illusion does not apply. Artificial Intelligence. CNNs will immediately recognize features in the face that are reverted and have no difficulty scanning an image that is upside down or upright. The reason is that CNNs will have seen far more images of human faces in their upright position, and stores all the features, shapes and subcomponents in their layers. Reversed eyes and mouth are unusual and whether a picture is upside down or not the CNN is not troubled with. Apparently human minds

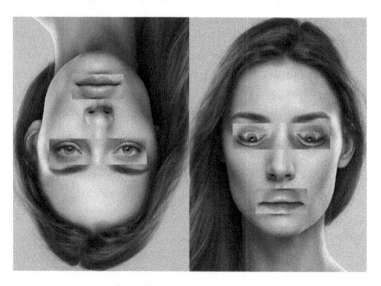

**Figure 7.2** Reverted face effect (in an AI generated picture).

process faces holistically, and this process is very different from the way artificial minds go about it.

## HOW DO HUMAN AND ARTIFICIAL MINDS HEAR?

Just as spectacularly the human mind processes light waves to visual information, it spectacularly processes sound waves to auditory information. Shifts of air molecules produce changes in air pressure, entering our ears through the auditory canal as sound waves, hitting the eardrum. The vibrations of the eardrum ultimately reach the tiny hair cells in the inner ear. These hair cells are the ear's version of the photoreceptors in the human eye. The hairs cells send information to the auditory nerves to the brain's auditory cortex. Just like the human eye translates physical (light wave) signals to neural information, the human ear does this for physical (sound wave) signals. And in case you were wondering whether the process really is that simple, indeed this description of the process of hearing is an oversimplification. But it will do for now.

Let's consider somebody talking to us. On first sight (or rather first sound) the process seems rather simple. We process each sound we hear to words and these words to sentences. And we give meaning to it. For instance, we hear ðˈəstˈʌfinˈoʊzjˈiːldztˈuːnˈoʊnˈuːɑːnsɪz. This is the International Phonetic alphabetic notation for sounds th-e-st-u-ff-y-n-ose-yield-s-to-no-nuances. Pretty simple: "the stuffy nose yields to no nuances." If speech recognition were only to be that simple! The problem is that we could have also heard "The stuff he knows yields two known nuances." And this makes recognizing speech for human minds and ears not as easy as it sounds. Sound combinations may yield different meanings. The clearest example is when the sound of a word links to different meanings, so called homophones. English has some 2,000 of them. Words that sound the same, but mean something different ("flower" and "flour", "bear" and "bare"). But there are also words that do not only sound the same but are written the same way, and yet have hundreds of different meanings (as "set" and "run" demonstrate; you can check your dictionary). Contrary to the recognition of printed sentences, the biggest problem with speech recognition is that. we. do. not. pause. between. words. when. we. speak. There is one big sound stream that the human mind needs to chunk into different words. And that is quite a challenge for human and artificial minds alike.

If I asked you at the beginning of this chapter what would be more difficult for artificial minds, recognizing images or recognizing speech, it is likely you voted for the former. Intuitively, automated speech recognition seems much simpler than automated image recognition. After all, computer vision deals with highly variable spatial data. Lighting, perspective, objects blocking other objects, interference from the image background, and understanding 3D structures from 2D data make image recognition extremely hard. Speech recognition "only" deals with some temporal data, and needs to recognize the temporal sequence of sounds that form words and sentences. Sure, it needs to account for different accents, speed rates, background noise, and emotions. But English "only" has 44 speech sounds (or phonemes). Twenty-seven letters in the alphabet and 44 speech sounds? That's right, as "ough" in "though", "tough", "dough", and "cough" demonstrates.

Despite the fact that automated speech recognition seems so viable, for a long time speech recognition systems had a very hard time to translate speech sounds into words. Whereas the enthusiasm in the 1980s suggested that it only was a matter of years to recognize speech, it took quite a bit more time. Only around 2010 the first speech recognition systems started to yield results that were encouraging. One of the reasons early speech recognition systems did rather poorly, had everything to do with the stuffy-nose (or "stuff he knows") example given earlier. That is, early systems used a statistical sequence prediction model.[10] As the speech recognition system listened to incoming speech, it used probabilities to guess the sequence sound that most likely formed the words given the sequence of sounds. And the word sounds to sentences. That turned out not to be enough. The breakthrough in speech recognition came with the advancements in deep learning[11]. The use of deep learning, specifically architectures such as Recurrent Neural Networks (RNNs) and Long Short-Term Memory (LSTM) networks, made a difference. They allowed for modelling longer-range dependencies in speech. With these models the story about a scientist who knows things could actually be distinguished from somebody with a stuffy nose.

Deep learning basically eliminated the need for separate AI models that first extracted features from speech to translate into letters and then formed these letters into words and later sentences. Instead, deep learning allowed the entire speech recognition system to learn from all aspects of the raw audio data bottom-up and top-down. Such a holistic approach turned out to be far more successful than a sequential approach. And that approach of artificial minds turned out to be more akin of the approach taken by human minds.

Today's AI models go well beyond understanding human speech. Artificial minds are now able to *generate* speech. You can train an artificial neural network with your own voice in only a few minutes. The different layers in the network capture the unique characteristics of your voice, and a speech synthesizer can then generate speech you have never expressed before with your exact voice. And if you thought you did not master speaking that one obscure foreign language? Well, according to the Generative AI model trained on your voice you now do.

It is not only speech auditory artificial minds recognize and generate. It is also able to recognize and classify music. And it is now even able to *generate* music. Glamour 80s rock about ducks in red rubber boots, or a soul song on stuffy noses can now be easily generated on the fly thanks to deep learning models. This generation process is very similar to that of image generation. After the deep learning model has been trained on large amounts of music, it has recognized patterns in different music styles. Diffusion models deconstruct songs with adding noise to the music, and then construct the song again by removing noise. The Judges Generator and Discriminator will take care of the rest, battling it out who creates the best sound, finetuning the quality of your musical piece. Before you know it, in addition to having become the next Van Gogh, you have become the next Mozart, Beethoven, Taylor Swift or The Beatles.

## HOW DO ARTIFICIAL MINDS OWN COPYRIGHTS?

In the late 20th century pop music, hip hop and electronic music underwent a revolution by sampling techniques. These samples, bits and pieces of one song, were used in another new song. There are instances of a sample of one specific song used in thousands of other songs[12]. It is obvious that the composer of the original song should be credited when parts of their song are used in a new song. It was their imagination that created the original song, so a new song using that imagination should credit the original imaginative sources. When AI creates new material, it also creates the new material from old material. In a way, it also uses samples, albeit that these samples can not directly be traced back to the original song. If I ask a music generator – Suno, MusicGen or Riffusion – to generate a soul song about the contents of this book (unlikely to be a major hit on the charts), it takes bits and pieces of existing soul music. Should James Brown or Prince be credited? If I ask an image generator – Dall-E, Midjourney, Gemini, Firefly – to generate a duck in rubber boots in Van Gogh style, should Van Gogh be credited? And what may be true for music and images, is then also true for text. A LLM trained on the style of George Orwell is able to generate an entirely new novel of that author on any topic. Including one where the main character is a duck in red rubber boots.

Companies that sell Generative AI are very aware of this copyright issue. Ask an image generator to create a picture of Tom Cruise in red rubber boots on a tricycle and the request cannot be completed because the request does not meet policies. Not so much the policies of not allowing famous actors in red rubber boots on tricycles, but the portrait rights of a specific actor. And ask a music generator to create music in the style of James Brown or Taylor Swift, and the same feedback is given. If the music is directly traceable to the Godfather of Soul and the new Queen of Pop, it violates policies. Instead, if it generates soul music or pop music untraceable to a specific artist albeit based on (their) existing music, a new song has arisen.

The question is whether Generative AI really violates copyrights. In a way it does, in a way it does not. When I am writing this book, I most certainly use words and phrases that I have seen and heard before. Of course, I am not allowed to plagiarize (just as composers were not allowed to use identifiable samples in their music) but the building blocks of the language I am using have definitely been used by somebody else before. Credits first and foremost go to my parents, both my biological and my academic ones. Following this logic, one can argue that any composer of a piece of music, any human composer, uses existing material. The very notes of a music piece have most certainly been used before. But the combination of those notes, preferably a rather unique combination, makes the music new. No matter how much inspiration that composer used from other material, if that new music is untraceable to an existing song, it is apparently not infringing on any copyrights.

An AI model that rebuilds an image or piece of music from visual or auditory white noise does that in an untraceable way. Just like human minds have read books, seen pictures and heard music to train their mental models, have artificial minds read books, seen pictures and heard music to train their models. Crediting the owners of this training material is impossible given the sheer amount of material the artificial model has actually been trained on to generate new material. Unless of course, other AI models do allow for tracing back the samples in the generated image, video or music to their rightful owner.

## HOW DO HUMAN AND ARTIFICIAL MINDS PERCEIVE TOUCH?

Temperature, pressure, vibration, pain. Haptic sensors detect them in our skin. Sensory neurons pick up these signals and send them through the spinal cord to the different areas in the brain. Human minds have quite a sensitive sense of touch. This is not surprising, as touch is needed for fine motor skills. And for texture discrimination. And for social bonding. You can ask your loved ones on the latter. We have areas on our body that have densely packed somatosensory receptors, such as our palm and our fingertips for precise tactile perception. But our face too is extremely sensitive. Our lips, cheeks and tongue can detect the gentlest touch. On the other hand, areas like our back, our legs, and our upper arms are far less sensitive to touch. The distribution of these receptors reflects the different roles the different areas on our body play in the interaction with the environment. By measuring the extent of the temperature, pressure, and vibration of an object we touch, human minds know whether we deal with danger or comfort. And when we touch something, we can usually also see that something, so vision and touch commonly go hand in hand.

For artificial minds something similar takes place. So-called triboelectric (for touch) and pyroelectric (for heat) sensors do the same as what somatosensory receptors do for humans. These sensors pick up different tactile sensations from the environment. And that turns out to be particularly useful for the wearer of those sensors. Meet the robot. By combining the visual object recognition and tactile senses, robots are able to operate in the world around us without squeezing an object too hard (for instance an orange) or too softly (for instance a door handle). By equipping robots with various visual and touch sensors, their artificial minds in their artificial bodies can perceive their surroundings and perform a range of complex tasks. They can run, climb, jump, fall, open doors and close them. All operated by, you guessed it, artificial neural networks that have been trained on perceiving the world around it, and on acting upon that world.

## HOW DO HUMAN AND ARTIFICIAL MINDS SMELL AND TASTE?

Different than vision, audition and touch that all operate on physical signals, the other two human senses, olfaction and taste, operate on chemical signals. When comparing the performance of these five senses in humans and non-human animals on a passing grade for A-levels, humans score a B for vision, a B for touch, a C for audition, a C for gustation, and a failing D for olfaction.

Olfaction is peculiar in many ways. It is the sense that has the most direct route to the human brain. When chemical particles enter our nose, odorant molecules come into contact with smell receptors, which transmit information to the olfactory bulb, the brain's smell centre. This direct connection to the brain emphasizes the importance of smell for our survival. But our failing grade on olfaction also tells us that humans apparently relied more on other senses than olfaction. Vision for instance, on which we perform better.

In gustation chemical substances from the food and liquid in our mouth dissolve with our saliva. Taste buds on our tongue, but also our mouth and throat, are the photoreceptors of gustation. We have some 10,000 taste buds that detect the five tastes: sweet, sour, salty, bitter and (most recently) umami. These taste buds transmit neural signals to the different areas of the brain. The magic in gustation is the sheer combination of parameters. It is not simply 5 x 5 combinations of tastes, but many subtle gradations of taste. And it is not only the combination of these tastes, but the combination with smell that adds to the combinations – thousands of different odours. Combined with the texture, temperature, and spiciness of food, and individual differences, we are dealing with a flavour explosion!

Can artificial minds also taste and smell, just like human minds? Given the evidence from vision and audition, and given the extensive discussion on the accomplishments of artificial neural networks, it can hardly be surprising that the answer is again affirmative. The problem here is less the information processing – the architecture of the artificial neural networks is pretty much the same for olfaction and gustation as they are for the other senses. The problem lies more in the E-nose and E-tongue that need to pick up the input signals, and the labelling of the input for supervised learning. Over the years chemical sensors have been developed. An E-tongue uses chemical sensors that are sensitive to different taste qualities, each sensor being sensitive to specific types of molecules. Similarly, an E-nose uses sensors that when they come into contact with a substance, they produce a change in electrical signals depending on the type and concentration of the molecules.

Of course, it is tempting to think of the ultimate perfume – particularly the one that attracts your preferred partner – or the ultimate wine – for that same romantic dinner while you wear that AI generated perfume. But the E-Tongues and E-noses still underperform. In today's world they are generally only applied as safety devices. On recognition. Trained on natural gas, the E-noses sniff for gas leaks. And trained on food quality the E-tongues can prevent you from eating spoilt food. The E-noses and E-tongues currently only perform well for the very specific signals they have been trained on. As with the early visual and auditory systems, the lack of training data – how do you label different tastes and smells? – is one of at least two problems.

The other problem touches upon the common theme in this book. There is quite a lot of psychology research on vision and audition. There is also quite a lot of AI research on vision and audition. Perhaps because psychology research still lacks a comprehensive understanding of olfaction and gustation, there remain too many questions for AI to provide answers to as well.

Let's conclude this chapter with what we started out with. A picture is more than a thousand words. And perhaps we can say the same for sounds, smells, tastes and touches. For human minds these sensory stimuli form features, which form shapes and components, which forms a template that we give meaning to. When considering perception in human minds, the perception process in artificial minds has hopefully become clearer.

# 8

---

# HOW DO HUMAN AND ARTIFICIAL MINDS COMPETE?

So far this book has described the many opportunities artificial minds have to offer. How artificial minds work, what their potential is, and what opportunities they offer. But what about all the harm artificial minds could do? Indeed, when we trust the media, a lot of harm awaits us. Our jobs will disappear because algorithms will do what we now do but faster, better and cheaper. Our privacy will be gone with AI linking large datasets so they can make high-probability predictions that will let others know more about ourselves than we do. AI is used for intelligent warfare, where the worst-case scenarios we only know from science fiction movies would become the harsh reality. It may even be the case that artificial minds become so intelligent that they decide there is no longer a need for humans in their (artificial) world. To end this book on a more positive note, let me try to put these circulating doom scenarios in a bit more perspective.[1]

## WHY DO HUMAN MINDS FEEL THREATENED BY ARTIFICIAL MINDS?

Let's hope not, but imagine one of your body parts – be it your knees, your hip, or one of your organs – fails to function and you were offered the opportunity to have it replaced by an artificial substitute.

For the sake of the discussion, any body part can be replaced with an artificial alternative flawlessly, and the alternative would function at least as well as the original. Would you have your knee replaced by an artificial knee? Your hip by an artificial hip? There is a high likelihood you would be fine with these options. Your heart? Maybe a bit more hesitant, but then again, a pacemaker may be agreeable to you. If you know for certain your artificial heart will function as well as the real one, you will likely be convinced to have it replaced in case of emergency. Now the key question: Imagine your brain fails. Would you be willing to have your brain replaced by an artificial entity? And if you know for certain your artificial brain would function as well as the real one? You are likely more squeamish about this option. But why?

The answer to that question might be the answer to the question why people are so much concerned with developments in AI. For millennia the human brain and human mind have been attributed to something sacred. Our brain and mind are somehow related to our soul. Plato described the human soul as reflections of eternal forms, with true knowledge and wisdom coming from the rational mind. Medieval Christian philosophy viewed the rational mind as a reflection of divine intellect that distinguished humans from animals. Descartes' *cogito, ergo sum* ("I think, therefore I am") shows the unique capabilities our mind offers. In short, the human mind is what makes *homo sapiens* (the thinking human) stand out. Literally. For decades we arrogantly convinced ourselves that animal cognition obviously did not come close to our outstanding human cognition[2]. And I will not even mention the possibility of plant cognition. Perhaps it is therefore not surprising that when a 'species', an artificial one nonetheless, shows humanlike thinking capabilities, our human intelligence feels threatened by some other form of intelligence, an artificial form.

## HOW DO HUMAN MINDS FEED ARTIFICIAL MINDS?

"Your call may be monitored for quality purposes." This is a friendly, polite and comprehensive way of the other side of your call stating:

> Anything you say, how you say it, why you say it, and who is saying it, will be used as input data to train our artificial neural networks in order for them to make better predictions on a variety of topics we will gladly not inform you about. Thanks for giving us all your free data to further automate our systems and become more profitable!

And don't worry (or do worry), AI models are collecting your data all over the place without you knowing it, or at least without you realizing it. Of course, whenever you are using the web, your browsing activities are recorded, and "trained for quality purposes". These input data are great for making predictions about you and people like you (and therefore people *not* like you). These data range from the websites you visit, how long you spend on those websites, what you click on, your mouse movements, your page scrolls, and your hovering over links. Cookies, trackers and scripts that are built in those websites are very grateful for you visiting them. Your activities on social media provide algorithms with even more valuable data. The pictures you upload, the language input you give, the people you befriend (and those you unfriend), what days and times you are (and are not) posting on social media, they all provide a very complete picture of who you are, and who people like you are. Even better, all these data serve as excellent input data for a range of AI algorithms that can be used for a large variety of purposes.

Of course, the input for deep learning models is by no means limited to your activities on the web. Your payment at your local store, the location of your smart phone, the health information from your smart watch, the cameras in your local town to ensure your safety, your smart doorbell, your television and all other entertainment you use, they all ensure a steady stream of valuable data that serve as valuable input for hungry AI algorithms. The AI models eagerly swallowing the incoming data are not only using unsupervised machine learning algorithms, but they can also use supervised learning algorithms, and even reinforcement learning algorithms. You are the perfect pigeon in a Skinner chamber called AI. You randomly watch a clip on the web, and the algorithm will reward you if you stay on, by giving you more of the fast clip food you like. You stay, the algorithm receives positive reinforcement; you leave, a penalty is given to the algorithm. Meanwhile the machine learning algorithms knows what you will like – after all, you don't click away – or do not like – when you do click away – so next time, the algorithms know perfectly well what makes you behave the way they like you to.

"Quality purposes" when using text messages and emails are equally rewarding. None of the email services will scan the exact content of your data according to the privacy regulations (at least they now say they do not do this anymore). But I hope you have carefully gone through the 10–15 pages of legal language before you digitally signed the agreement by clicking to agree. The attachments of your email are carefully scanned (for viruses), but the sender and recipient information, the date and time of the email, subject lines, whether the email has been opened or not, and the links you clicked within the email are equally rewarding as the content of your email. After all, no machine learning algorithm is really interested in the exact information of you as an individual. But the algorithms are extremely interested in more (and more) data to better predict the outcome of the model for your kind of people.

The type of data that gets collected is diverse. Algorithms love diverse data, because their predictions can become even better. Imagine that your fitness tracker shows a decline in physical activity. Your smart phone – which already knows when you go to sleep and wake up because of its (in)activity– starts to detect that you use your phone in the middle of the night. Your uploaded social media pictures do not show the colourful content they did before. Your social media posts contain language that is different from the language you used before. Your web browsing activities show you are searching for articles on burnout. Your payment history suggests an increased interest in that bottle of wine. And the email messages you send show you are contacting fewer people. You don't have to be a powerful artificial neural network to make some pretty good predictions based on data that may *seem* rather innocent when not considered collectively.

It is not just the diversity of data that has grown over the years, it is also the amount of data. Massive amounts of data are collected each day. If we only consider some of the activities on the web, we share over 8,500 Snapchat photos and post the same number of messages! We watch almost 85,000 YouTube videos! We send 2.5 million emails! And we do that per second. That's right. Per second! These massive amounts of data are priceless for training deep learning models, because they contain the input data – the information we send around – as well as the output data (every little move you do, or do not, make is valuable feedback for the network).

Supermarkets can run convenient experiments on you. They change the location of an item in your local supermarket and the prediction models – knowing the output in terms of sales – can predict whether this is empirically the best place for that product. Or let me give another example. Your car navigation system can predict the fastest route based on the input data from all the other drivers that are on the road. The human mind of a German artist successfully fooled the artificial mind called Google. He single-handedly created a traffic jam on Google Maps by walking around with 99 used cell phones. The Google Maps algorithm immediately predicted so much traffic on one location that it marked a major traffic jam. Yet the artist strolled along the small German road pulling a cart with the cell phones happily sending out their location data[3].

We feed artificial neural networks with our data. Our text data, our location data. Our physiological data. Our financial data. And with more data and with sufficient computational power these deep learning models can become increasingly more 'intelligent'. Every apocalypse scenario from any science fiction movie has pretty much been covered in the media. So much so, that the end seems near.

## THE END IS NEAR

Current AI models are deeply impressive in their performance: ask them to write a sonnet given some keywords and the system is able to generate a sonnet as an artificial Shakespeare; ask a song in glamorous 80s rock and the next Top of the Pops hit is a fact; ask for a painting on people communicating with virtual reality glasses in Van Gogh style and a modern "Potato Eaters" has been created. But then think about the fact that the parameters in these models are still 100,000 times less complex than those in the human brain. And that the human brain "was trained" on 4,000 times more data than for instance a model such as ChatGPT-4 was ever trained on.[4] More data in terms of volumes of data, but also in terms of more diverse data. That is comforting in the sense that the most accomplished artificial mind thus still seems far away from approximating the complexity of the human mind.

But the difference between human and artificial minds is worrisome at the same time. Over the last two years alone 90 percent of the data in the world was generated. The 3.7 billion humans that use the internet generate some 2,500,000 terabytes of data every day[5]. That means that it is a matter of time – a year or so – to have reached the estimated amount of input data for artificial minds that human minds have gathered over a lifetime. These are of course only approximations, but it does make one wonder what would happen if AI models were trained on 4,000 times more data than they currently are.

The amount of data may be alarming, but the limited computing power should at least reduce the worry. Artificial neural networks with more hidden layers than the current 96 in the most sophisticated models need so much more computing power, that this will undoubtedly form a bottleneck for AI to reach humanlike performance[6]. That bottleneck at least makes sure that the end is near not yet. However, time will tell. A few years before Gordon Moore founded the Intel corporation, in 1965 he made a prediction that is now known as Moore's Law. This law states that the number of transistors per integrated circuit doubles every year. Computers would continuously become more powerful. Moore's Law still applies today, even though the time for the number of transistors to double is taking a bit longer than the strict interpretation of the law predicts. Moore made his prediction when there were only 64 transistors in a chip. Today we count about 50,000,000,000 transistors, pretty much as was predicted. And Moore's Law will undoubtedly be revised when quantum computers enter the stage, computers that leverage the principles of quantum mechanics. Rather than handling information as either a 0 or 1 as the computers as we know it do, quantum computers use quantum bits or qubits[7], yielding an expected quadratic speedup for specific tasks. A task is predicted to take approximately the square root of the time that same task now takes.

With a large enough artificial neural network, with a large enough number of hidden layers, with enough computational power, with enough feedback to train the model and with enough trial and error, it becomes very likely the best (or worst) is yet to come. Some say it then becomes very likely we reach singularity, a point in the not so far away future where artificial minds become more intelligent, far more intelligent than human minds. A future in which artificial minds communicate in a way we do no longer understand, with a network complexity incomprehensible to us. Some visionaries have long predicted (or advocated) singularity, instilling the fear in others than machines will take over the world.

Now, we can insistently argue that we designed the "bloody thing" and therefore can always keep control over what it does. The problem is that this is no longer true. We have only set up the architecture. We have very little control over the learning processes and the evolution of these artificial minds. We even have less control over the data we feed these algorithms, given the sheer amount of data and the diversity of data sources. Most LLM models now allow you to write computer code in your favourite programming language. But now imagine we no longer understand the mechanisms of LLMs. Computer code incomprehensible to human minds gets rewritten by AI because that code happens to be more convenient than the computer code it used at its inception. If we do no longer have any insight into the code, we no longer understand the code, and no longer have control over that code. Consequently, we no longer understand the machine's decisions.

A world dominated by AI. A world in which autonomous battlefield robots surpass human military power. A world in which fake news in simulated environments bias us in every direction it – the system, a continent, a country, The Matrix – wants us to be directed in. A world in which free will is something we can only think back to with nostalgia. A world in which artificial minds predict every breath you take. Every move you make. Every vow you break. Every smile you fake, and every claim you stake. It is watching you[8].

## SHOULD AI BE STOPPED?

In 2023, the year that Open AI impressed the world with ChatGPT and Dall-E, a petition was launched to halt AI. Some 30,000 people signed the petition that called on "all AI labs to immediately pause for at least 6 months the training of AI systems more powerful than GPT-4." The petition received lots of attention in the media, as it exemplified our deepest fears for artificial minds taking over our world.

But what was meant by "all AI Labs"? Would AI Labs include my own research lab and that of many of my colleagues? Or would the focus be on the really large non-academic research labs that Big Tech companies ran, which tend to be less transparent, because they do not have to be transparent? Would it include the AI Labs that are working on a cure for that deadly disease many of us are suffering from? And would all AI labs also include all governmental agencies, including the defence agencies that protect us? Would all AI labs concern all labs worldwide, or only those in some parts of the world, and if so, which parts? How could one even monitor all AI labs worldwide?

Even if we were to be able to define all AI labs and pause train-ing of systems to prevent further harm, would 6 months really be enough? Should a pause of 6 years (or perhaps 60 years) be called for instead? How would we decide on the time frame of the pause beforehand, and would we not only be able to determine the most appropriate duration of the time frame in hindsight? Should we only pause AI systems more powerful than GPT-4 (in which case it is assumed the current systems do not pose any harm)? Or should we erase well over 70 years of research and development that led to these very systems? Would we allow for the architectures such as GPT-4 to be paused, but the training data for these networks be continued to be fed, so these "old" systems can continue to be used for training? Would we perhaps be allowed to not develop single AI systems more powerful than GPT-4, but are we allowed to build a system that configures an ensemble of GPT-4 systems? And when does a system become more powerful than GPT-4? When it runs faster? When is it trained on more data? When it becomes more accurate and reliable? Or when its artificial mind approaches the capacities of our human mind?

And why is it that representatives from Big Tech signed the petition? Why do they caution us against the dangers of AI? If anybody could really pause AI, then it is Big Tech that is currently developing the very systems that presumably endanger humanity. "Do not do unto others what you would not want done to yourself" seems to apply here.

These questions, the large number of them, are very relevant when truly understanding the threats AI potentially poses. I would strongly argue that not addressing these questions may very likely has the very opposite effect of what the signatories of the petition intended.

Regulation seems to be the key to constrain unwanted AI excesses. In 2024 the European Union adopted the world's first comprehensive AI law. It aimed for AI to be safe, transparent, traceable, non-discriminatory and environmentally friendly. It sought to find regulation to prevent AI models to generate illegal content, to use copyrighted data for training AI models, and to always enforce to disclose that content was generated by AI. Regulation is good, but global regulation is better. Nowadays you commonly hear: "For hardware you go to China, for software you go to the United States. For regulation you go to Europe." The good news is that at least one continent takes regulation very seriously to protect its citizens, their privacy and their freedom. The bad news is that if the problem is not addressed by *everybody* at the AI regulatory table, the problem really does not get addressed. The issue of course is who gets at the table? If parties at the regulatory table are Big Tech — as they are the ones who can afford it — the regulatory measures may be swayed to a specific (commercial) direction. And those countries not at the AI regulatory table may exactly be the countries for whom AI regulation ought to apply most. In all fairness, developments in AI cannot be stopped. However, its progress can be monitored and regulated. Globally.

## IS WORK GONE?

Economist John Keynes stated almost a century ago:

> We are being afflicted with a new disease of which some readers may not yet have heard the name, but of which they will hear a great deal in the years to come – namely, technological unemployment. This means unemployment due to our discovery of means of economising the use of labour outrunning the pace at which we can find new uses for labour.[9]

Today, this technological unemployment seems a fact. Our jobs will be taken over by AI. AI systems are able to handle tasks like bookkeeping and analysing financial data, and make accurate predictions for investments and risk management. Machines as accountants, auditors and financial analyst. With self-checkout machines and automated payment systems cashiers may not be needed, and chatbots and virtual humans may replace sales associates and receptionists. AI driven (self-driving) vehicles will serve as the artificial version of human truck drivers, taxi drivers, bus drivers, train drivers. AI will be able to do tasks now reserved for human journalists, content writers and video editors. There is hardly any area – from healthcare to legal, from professional services to education – where AI will not have a major impact. But the question is whether AI will take over our jobs so that we will be unemployed.

Over the last two centuries we have seen multiple technological revolutions. The first one was the Industrial Revolution at the end of the 18th century with mechanization. Coal along with the invention of the steam engine triggered a range of technological innovations. A century later the Second Industrial revolution followed, with massive technological advancements in a new source of energy – electricity, gas, and oil. Methods of communication such as the telegraph and the telephone emerged, as well as methods of transportation, including the automobile and the airplane. The Third Industrial Revolution, better known as the Digital Revolution, happened around the age AI was born, in the 1960s. Electronics, telecommunications and personal computers emerged, and space expeditions and biotechnology became possible. And two decades ago, we experienced a Fourth Revolution, with the accessibility to the internet. We may disagree whether we recently really experienced a fourth Industrial Revolution (or whether we have even entered a fifth), but fact is that thanks to the internet massive amounts of training data have become available for massive artificial neural networks that operate in internet-based cloud solutions.

With the advancements in AI, the threat of AI taking over our jobs has frequently been voiced. This may be true. But history sometimes is a good predictor of the future. When we look at the hours we work per week, the 2nd and 3rd Industrial Revolution do not show a major drop in working hours. Mapped out over time, we see that the number of hours we work per week has linearly decreased over time, and a major drop can be found around the 1940s, but there is no sign that any of the Industrial Revolutions have made a major difference to our working hours. Similarly, we have been paid linearly more over time, but the Industrial Revolutions have not affected this much, let alone for the worse. It is of course true that the kind of work has changed, undoubtedly because of the Industrial Revolutions that took place. The same may apply for the AI revolution. Indeed, jobs will likely change, as they have changed since the First Industrial Revolution. But it is not certain machines will eliminate our jobs. Based on the past, it is more likely humans will adapt to AI technologies, so that human minds work alongside artificial minds.

I am no fortune teller. I do not know whether we will become unemployed. But if all technological revolutions so far have not affected employment drastically, what gives the absolute certainty the current technological revolution does?

The quote by economist John Keynes this section started out with, did not end with pessimism. It continued:

> But this is only a temporary phase of maladjustment. All this means in the long run that mankind is solving its economic problem. I would predict that the standard of life in progressive countries one hundred years hence will be between four and eight times as high as it is to-day. There would be nothing surprising in this even in the light of our present knowledge. It would not be foolish to contemplate the possibility of a far greater progress still.

The argument posed almost a century ago seems to apply also today.

## IS SOCIETY GONE?

Due to AI our society will never be the same again! Virtual reality will make us homebound. Automated food deliveries will make us lazy and obese. We will not read or write anymore because AI technologies have taken over those creative skills too. Perhaps.

Perhaps the end of society as we know it is near. I cannot rule it out. But mind you, we feared something similar 150 years ago. An article in 1876 in the New York Times stated, "Thus the telephone, by bringing music and ministers into every home, will empty the concert-halls and the churches."[10] It did not quite happen, at least with regards to the concert-halls. And an article in the same newspaper one year later definitely announced the end of the world:

> The telephone was justly regarded as an ingenious invention when it was first brought before the public, but it is destined to be entirely eclipsed by the new invention or the phonograph. The former transmitted sound. The latter bottles it up for future use.[11]

Despite the invention of telephone and telegraph 150 years ago, we still talk, and we still go to concerts.

Undoubtedly society will change as it has always changed. Perhaps for the worst. But why *necessarily* for the worst? We now have cars, public transport, and airplanes, but we still like to hike, cycle, run, and walk. We have computer and television, but still like to go to concerts, theatres and cinemas. And even though we could meet in a conference call (as much as we do), we still prefer to meet in person, in the office, or in the pub.

But if AI may not affect how we operate in daily life, then certainly it affects how we are informed in daily life. AI will erase the boundaries of what is real and what is not. We can no longer trust any news outlet, because generative AI will have created information – text, pictures or video, or will have manipulated actual information so that fake news inundates our living rooms. It is undoubtedly true that generative AI creates content that is increasingly hard to distinguish from actual content. Deep fakes generated by deep learning models. But here too, throughout history, governments and media outlets have always used fake news to influence public opinion, start wars, or gain political power. Over many centuries politicians have changed their stories to convey to their voters the message that allowed them to stay in power. Rumours get spread, pictures get manipulated.

Meanwhile smarter AI algorithms *also* allow for distinguishing between what is real and what is fake. Measures are now in place to watermark AI generated pictures in order to make the difference between real and fake more detectable. For text it may be more difficult to detect this difference, but here too looks are deceiving. For instance, our understanding of LLMs allow us to also recognize texts created by Generative AI. Current automated detector systems are good at picking up whether a text is generated by AI or not.[12] And the moment AI systems have become better to fool AI detectors, new AI detectors are trained to repeat the cycle, so that Generative AI will become smarter, while the detection systems become even smarter.

## IS EDUCATION GONE?

Our educational system will be taken over by AI! Teachers will be replaced by intelligent tutoring systems that provide personalized education 24 hours a day, 7 days a week. These tutoring systems monitor the learning processes of their students, and continuously adapt themselves to a student's performance so that each individual student receives the most optimal education. Students will no longer think, but will have their essays written by the most sophisticated Natural Language Processing algorithms. Writing is no longer thinking; instead, it is entering the best prompt into the algorithm, so that it produces the most optimal essay. The task has now become how to best play the AI system. Once the essays have been written, similar Natural Language Processing algorithms score these essays on their performance. It no longer is an evaluation of a student, but a battle of the machines.

There are a number of responses to this grim scenario. There is every reason we may want to consider changes in our educational system – a system that has not quite kept up with the societal changes we have been facing over the last decades, or even the last centuries. Is personalized learning with a 24/7 personal tutor that can guide the learner in the process and helps out when needed an ideal scenario? The current teaching work force will not now, and unlikely ever, be able to provide such personalized education. There will always be more students than teachers. If custom-made personalized learning is important, we will have to rely on AI.

Of course, changes in our educational system do not necessarily need to include AI. But they could very well. The question then is how passionate teaching by human minds can work along with teaching by artificial minds. Even if it turns out that a skill that may now be taken over by AI, for instance essay writing skills, is critical for a successful future – as I think writing skills are – job selection will ultimately take place based on that skill. Consequently, education will have to teach that skill to a younger generation. Perhaps job interviews will change, testing applicants on their very writing skills (or on their prompting skills). And finally, no matter how much we may want to control students not to use available AI technologies, that control will fade over time. After all, calculators are no longer banned from math classes. Dictionaries are often allowed at exams. Better to look at the "problem" long-term rather than short-term.

As with the other examples given in this chapter, we can also turn the argument around: if society is changing due to the developments in AI, with our younger generation growing up in this AI-driven society, should the educational system then not adapt as to better prepare our younger generation for a future that includes AI?

## IS SAFETY GONE?

Imagine a fully autonomous unmanned aerial vehicle, better known as a drone, takes off. Without any human intervention possible it decides itself when it is ready to release its load. A bomb. These autonomous drones can bomb cities and do that without human intervention. When it comes to AI-driven warfare there is even more reason to be concerned, as this concern has been fuelled by many years of science fiction movies. To many this truly is a horror scenario. Indeed, it may be.

But here too I would like to present a flipside to the discussion. What if these autonomous drones were to only reach military targets with the highest precision. They would no longer cause any collateral damage. In today's warfare mistakes are made, frequently and widely. Civilians are sacrificed in military warfare, in part because when human minds operate weapons, they are not as precise, consistent, and errorless as when artificial minds do. Autonomous warfare aircrafts are not what we should desire. Rather, I would very much be in favour of banning all warfare across the world. But also, recent history has shown us this is pretty much an illusion. If autonomous warfare means that AI systems of one country are fighting with AI systems of another country, it might put things in a very different perspective. In addition, that would demonstrate how pointless the very concept of war is.

Imagine I had started this section on safety differently. Let me try again.

Imagine a fully autonomous drone that takes off and, without any human intervention, possibly decides itself when it is ready to release its load. Medical and food supplies. With the highest precision these autonomous drones reach their intended targets with the highest precision. People in dire need of medical help and food can be reached thanks to these AI-driven devices. Whereas human minds make mistakes in reaching target groups, artificial minds would reach those in need most effectively.

Would such a start of this section change your view on using these autonomous drones?

There are many examples in history of technological advancements, where funding from defence departments led to progress initially not intended for defence purposes. The Advanced Research Projects Agency Network (ARPANET) in the 1960s started out to enable resource sharing between remote computers and formed the technical foundation of what we now know as the internet. Chemical research intended for industrial or agricultural improvements led to mustard gas and chlorine gas ultimately used for military purposes. Chemical compounds initially studied for medical purposes to develop new medications, led to the creation of nerve agents like Sarin. All scientific and technological developments, including AI could be used for military purposes. But rather than banning artificial minds altogether, perhaps we should consider the following: Creating better humans will always be more important than creating smarter machines[13].

## DOES AI CHANGE WITH THE SEASONS?

It is not my aim to surprise or shock you – but the simplest way I can summarize is to say that there are now in the world machines that think, that learn and that create. Moreover, their ability to do these things is going to increase rapidly until – in a visible future – the range of problems they can handle will be coextensive with the range to which the human mind has been applied.

This quote comes from Herb Simon, one of the attendants of both the Dartmouth workshop and the MIT workshop. Words expressed about 70 years ago.

Since the 1960s, AI has had various "AI winter." Periods during which the expectations of what AI had to offer were followed by periods during which AI did not match these expectations and consequently research funding was reduced. The history of AI has known two major winters in the 1970s and the 1990s, as well as several smaller ones. The first AI winter started around the same time on both sides of the ocean. The increased tension between the United States and the Soviet Unition asked for quickly translating Russian documents into English, particularly military documents. At the time AI researchers were convinced that rule-based systems would make this possible, and US government heavily funded such machine translation research. The National Science Foundation commissioned an Automatic Language Processing Advisory Committee, including linguists and psychologists, which concluded automated machine translation was still something of the future. The disillusionment with the progress in AI led to major funding cuts.

Meanwhile, on the other side of the ocean the British Science Research Council evaluated academic research in the field of artificial intelligence (AI) following a conflict in one of the biggest centres for AI research in the country, the Department of Artificial Intelligence at the University of Edinburgh. The 1973 report stated: "In no part of the field have the discoveries made so far produced the major impact that was then promised".

The major setbacks that led to the AI winter can easily be explained in hindsight. Limitations of the hardware and software made AI systems struggle with problems that required large amounts of memory and processing power. What was doable in small-scaled problems, turned out to be harder in when scaling up to real-world applications.

The second AI winter occurred after a revival of AI interest in the early 1980s. After the first AI winter AI companies realized that rule-based systems, symbolic AI, may not be the solution to all problems AI aimed to solve, but were very useful for expert systems. AI systems should not aim for general problem solvers but specific problem solvers. Again, expectations at the time spiralled out of control. As with the inflated expectations that led to the first AI winter, disappointment kicked in when researchers realized these systems were difficult to scale-up. Scaling up rule-based systems is notoriously hard and therefore expensive. Moreover, these intelligent systems did not know how to go about new and unforeseen cases outside the predefined rules.

The primary reason that led to the two major (and a series of smaller) AI winters was the out-of-control inflated expectations what AI could offer. The other reason was the limited computing power, and the limited amount of data AI systems could be trained on. Today, the second reason seems to have been taken away. Thanks to our information society, there are no limitations on available data to train systems (and if there are, it is a matter of time for these data too are in place). Given the many cloud solutions, computing power does not seem to be a major limitation anymore. However, such optimism was also demonstrated just before the two AI winters arrived. The first reason therefore applies also today: inflated expectations of what AI can and will do should be considered with a healthy dose of caution. The AI fox should not be caught trice in the same snare.

## THE END IS NEAR, BUT THE BEGINNING IS CLOSER

My goal in this final chapter has not been to trivialize the potential threats society faces with a technological revolution. Any technological revolution, including one called AI. Instead, my goal has been to place potential threats in perspective by showing similar situations from the past. When the end is near and the beginning is closer, what does the future of AI have in store for us? Solid predictions made over several decades have been off by at least 50 years (and given the fact that the clock is still ticking likely much longer).

The intelligence of artificial intelligence. Throughout this book it should have become clear that we do not really know how to best define intelligence. Concepts such as Artificial General Intelligence (AGI) or singularity are therefore fascinating, but very elusive. Whereas the former matches human intelligence, and the second even surpasses it, we do not quite know what intelligence entails in the first place. After all, we don't even have a good grasp of human intelligence. Is it only human intelligence in terms of reasoning and thinking, or does it also extend to emotional and social intelligence? And are we constrained by human intelligence, or should we also consider the outstanding navigational intelligence exhibited by migrating birds, and aquatic mammals and fish? The outstanding olfactory intelligence exhibited by dogs and rats? The outstanding evolutionary intelligence exhibited by ants and cockroaches? The irony is that the question whether Artificial General Intelligence, an intelligence that matches human intelligence, has been reached, has been asked frequently. The opposite question is hardly ever voiced: when will human intelligence match artificial intelligence? If that question is asked, it is likely that somebody will respond asking: "Hey now, what kind of intelligence do you refer to?"

Once the question is addressed what kind of intelligence we are talking about, we will have to consider the different levels of analysis. Does an AI system that solves the same problem humans aim to solve approach human intelligence? Or should the system to be considered human intelligent also use the same mechanisms as humans use to solve the problem? And in doing this, should AI use the same apparatus – a humanlike brain – or will only similarities in the mechanisms suffice? These questions become particularly important because human minds are eager to anthropomorphize the world around us. If it *seems* to act like a human, it must be humanlike. How pleased we are when our device welcomes us when we switch it on and says goodbye when we shut it down! In other words, a system may *look* intelligent while it really is not, and it may *be* intelligent while it does not look like it through our human eyes.

Today there is every reason to be excited by the opportunities AI has to offer. Yet, what the AI winters have shown is that hot summers of genuine enthusiasm led to winters where interest and funding decreased. No matter how hard we exclaim that this time things are different, that this time AI truly is intelligent, it is worth remembering that several times in the past a very similar conclusion was drawn. History does not always repeat itself, but it is worth keeping the past in mind.

AI winters occurred in part because of a misunderstanding regarding the difference between basic fundamental and applied industrial research. Basic research can become applied, but sometimes this transition takes considerably longer than what one had hoped for. The excitement at the time about basic research did not immediately translate in excitement regarding the application of such research, which led to funding cuts in basic research. These cuts in turn led to further delays in applied research. The problem is that the only difference between basic research and applied research is time. Early technology readiness levels in basic research are needed for higher technology readiness levels that lead to an application. Not understanding the value of basic research, or being impatient about its applications, hinders progress and leads to disappointments (and AI winters).

Many of the disappointments in the development of AI originated in the inability of AI systems to scale up. Symbolic AI seemed great for small-scale problems, but when the problems became real, these systems required major overhauls. Goodbye good old-fashioned AI and welcome Modern AI. A Modern AI where artificial neural networks learn patterns and can handle new unseen data and make better predictions. The advantages of modern AI are clear. And yet, modern AI excels at recall but not always at precision, whereas good old-fashioned AI excelled at precision, but not so much on performance. Taking both approaches into account seems wise, as Symbolic AI and Modern AI can very well be complementary.

Artificial intelligence started out and has always been a very inter-disciplinary field. AI researchers have often been trained as psychologists. That was then, and this is now. In 2024 the Nobel Prize in Physics was awarded to physicist John Hopfield, known for a type of artificial neural network named after him (the Hopfield network) and cognitive psychologist and computer scientist Geoffrey Hinton, who is affectionally called "the Godfather of AI". That same year the Nobel Prize in Chemistry was awarded to biochemist and computational biologist David Baker, chemist and computer scientist John Jumper, and neuroscientist and artificial intelligence researcher Demis Hassabis. As we have seen throughout this book, developments in artificial intelligence have heavily relied on ideas formed in neuroscience and cognitive psychology. I hope it will remain doing that.

Again, I am no fortune teller. I can't tell where the future of AI will bring us. Whether the end is near or, which to me seems more likely, the beginning is closer. I do hope that the direction AI will continue to take is that of Explainable artificial intelligence (XAI). As a colleague of mine stated a few years ago:

> Within the Cognitive Sciences, we have been consider-ably more sceptical of big data's promise, largely because we place such a high value on explanation over prediction. A core goal of any cognitive scientist is to fully understand the system under investigation, rather than being satisfied with a simple descriptive or predictive theory.[14]

Rather than simply building smart artificial minds, it becomes increasingly important to comprehend the mechanisms of an AI model and therefore to better be able to trust its results. Particularly when it comes to deep learning models with many hidden layers, these AI models get reduced to a "black box" impossible to interpret. Explainability ensures that we have insight in the system. Consequently, we can determine whether the system works as expected. And it can help in determining whether the system matches the regulatory standards that have been defined, or inform how to best create these regulatory standards. It is fields such as psychology that have always emphasized explanations, and these explanations have formed the very foundations of artificial intelligence.

Human minds prefer familiar, predictable situations, and when faced with something new or poorly understood, they experience discomfort and anxiety. Human minds tend to avoid situations where the outcomes are uncertain. Just as ancient human minds feared thunder and lightning because they couldn't understand it, many of today's human minds fear complex phenomena like AI. Anxiety that arises from the unknown. The most effective way to deal with the cause of this anxiety is to make the phenomenon less mysterious. I hope this book has done exactly that. I am convinced that much of the fear in many of us about the threats of AI stem from many of us not knowing AI. In line with the title of this book, probably the best way to understand an artificial mind is to understand the human mind. And vice versa.

# GLOSSARY

**Accuracy:** A measure of how correctly a machine learning model performs, calculated as the ratio of correct predictions to the total number of predictions. Most common measure of performance.

**AI effect:** The phenomenon of downplaying an AI achievement, after long considering that very achievement as approaching human intelligence. As if moving the finish line during a race.

**AI winter:** A period of reduced funding and interest in AI research due to disappointing results and deliverables. These winters often follow 'summers' that mark overly heightened expectations.

**Algorithm:** A set of rules or steps to solve a problem especially by a computer.

**Anthropomorphize:** Attributing human-like characteristics to non-humans, including animals and machines.

**Arbitrariness:** The absence of a connection between (the sound of) a linguistic symbol and its meaning. If there only is an arbitrary connection between symbol and meaning, computers can never capture meaning like humans (see also *Chinese Room argument*).

**Artificial General Intelligence (AGI):** AI systems that possess the ability to understand, learn, and apply intelligence across a wide range of tasks, at the level of human cognitive abilities.

**Artificial intelligence (field):** The research field in computer science and/or cognitive science that focuses on creating machines that can perform and learn tasks similar to those performed by human intelligence.

**Artificial intelligence (technology):** "Smart" technologies that enable computers to perform and learn a variety of advanced functions presumably akin to human intelligence.

**Artificial neural network:** Computational models inspired by the structure of the brain, used for pattern recognition and learning, typically including input, output, and a series of hidden layers. (see also *Deep Learning, Connectionism,* and *Parallel Distributed Processing*).

**Backpropagation:** A training algorithm for artificial neural networks that compares the expected output to the actual output, and over time reduces the error between the two by propagating a correction to these errors by adjusting the weights between nodes backward through the network.

**Central Processing Unit (CPU)** : The primary hardware component of a computer responsible for executing instructions and performing basic arithmetic, logic, control, and input/output operations.

**Chinese Room argument:** A thought experiment proposed by philosopher John Searle addressing whether symbol manipulation only can constitute meaning, thereby criticizing artificial intelligence in general and natural language processing and computational linguistics specifically (see also *Arbitrariness*).

**Cognition:** The mental processes involved in acquiring knowledge and understanding, including thinking, memory, language, and problem-solving.

**Cognitive revolution:** A shift in psychology in the late 1950s that emphasized the study of the mind and mental processes, and the appeal of considering mental processes as computational processes.

**Computational Linguistics:** The study of using computational methods to analyse and model human language (also called *Natural Language Processing*).

**Connectionism:** An approach in cognitive science that models mental or behavioural phenomena using artificial neural networks. Also called *Parallel Distributed Processing* and *Deep Learning* (see also *Artificial Neural Networks*).

**Convolutional Neural Network (CNN):** A type of neural network often and ideally used in image recognition and processing by using convolutional layers.

**Data-driven:** Bottom-up approaches that starts from the datasets without a theory driving the analysis. Opposite of *Theory-driven*.

**Deep learning:** A subset of machine learning that uses multi-layered artificial neural networks to learn complex patterns in data. Also called *Connectionism, Parallel Distributed Processing* (see also *Artificial Neural Networks*).

**Distributional Semantics:** A linguistic approach where word meanings are derived from their distribution across contexts in large text corpora. Based on the idea that you know the meaning of a word by the company it keeps. Also called *Word Embedding*.

**Explainable AI (XAI):** AI systems whose decisions and processes are transparent and understandable, ensuring accountability and trust in their outputs.

**Fuzzy logic:** A form of logic that allows for reasoning with degrees of truth rather than binary true/false values, thereby creating more flexibility in an otherwise overly rigid logic system.

**Generative Adversarial Network (GAN):** A machine learning model where two neural networks, a generator and a discriminator, compete with each other to create realistic data.

**Generative AI:** AI models that learn patterns from existing data to create entirely new content, including text, images, text, and music.

**Goal state:** A desired outcome or end condition in problem-solving for AI algorithms.

**Good old-fashioned AI:** An approach to AI that emphasizes symbolic reasoning and rule-based systems. Always gives correct results, but very difficult to scale up. Also called *Symbolic AI*.

**Gut feeling:** An instinctive or intuitive feeling, often lacking rational explanation, that allows humans to think fast and good-enough.

**Hallucination:** Consequence of when a deep learning model generates incorrect, nonsensical, or misleading information.

**Hebbian learning:** A learning principle stating that neurons that fire together, wire together, strengthening their connections. Principle is named after Donald Hebb and applies to both human and artificial neural networks.

**Hidden layers:** Non-transparent layers in a neural network between the input and output layers where complex representations are learned. The higher the number of (hidden) layers, the more complex the network requiring more input data and computing power.

**Hidden–Markov Model (HMM):** A statistical model used to represent systems that have hidden (unobserved) states and observable outputs, often applied in sequence analysis and speech recognition.

**Image recognition:** The process of identifying objects, patterns, or features in images using computer vision and AI.

**Industrial revolution:** A period of major industrialization and digitization that transformed economies and societies over the centuries. Four industrial revolutions have been distinguished due to advances in coal, gas, electronics and nuclear, and the internet and renewable energy.

**Information Processing:** The theory that the human mind processes information in stages, similar to how a computer operates.

**Input units:** The neurons or nodes in an artificial neural network that receive initial data to process. Aim of the network is to process input units to output units.

**Intelligence:** The ability to learn, understand, and apply knowledge and skills to adapt to new situations, both in humans (human intelligence) and in machines (artificial intelligence). The exact definition what this ability entails is evasive.

**Knowledge representation:** Techniques for encoding information about the world in a format that a computer system can use to solve complex problems. Often propositional networks are used for this purpose, both in cognitive psychology and artificial intelligence.

**Large Language Models (LLM):** Artificial neural networks trained on extremely large amounts of text data to detect patterns that allow them to understand, reason through, and generate human-like language.

**Machine learning:** A subset of AI that enables computers to learn from data and improve their performance over time without being explicitly programmed. Different machine learning algorithms are available that excel at different tasks.

**Marr's tri-level hypothesis:** A framework proposing that cognitive processes can be understood at three levels: computational or rational, algorithmic or information processing, and implementational or biological level. Also called the why (the problem), the what (the rules) and the how (the physical system). Proposed by neuroscientist David Marr.

**Mentalese:** A theoretical "language of thought" in which cognitive processes are assumed to occur. Because language is imprecise, a language of thought cannot be human language but is presumed similar to it.

**Moore's Law:** The observation that the number of transistors on a microchip doubles approximately every two years, leading to exponential growth in computing power.

**Moravec paradox:** The observation that tasks requiring high-level reasoning are easier for computers than tasks that humans find simple, like perception and motor skills.

**Natural Language Processing (NLP):** The field of AI focused on enabling computers to understand, interpret, and generate human language. Also called *Computational Linguistics*.

**Neural networks:** Models inspired by the structure of biological brains, used for learning patterns and making decisions. See also *Artificial Neural Networks*.

**Operant conditioning** : human learning process in which behaviours are shaped and maintained by their consequences, such as rewards or punishments (see also *Reinforcement Learning*).

**Output units:** The neurons or nodes in an artificial neural network that produce the final result after processing input through hidden layers.

**Parallel Distributed Processing:** A model of cognitive processing in which information is processed simultaneously across multiple interconnected units connecting input units to output units through hidden layers in parallel. See also *Deep Learning, Connectionism*.

**Patterns of activation:** The specific responses of neurons in human and artificial neural networks when waves of information are stimulated in parallel.

**Precision:** Measurement of the proportion of true positive predictions among all positive predictions made by a model.

**Propositional logic:** A branch of logic dealing with propositions that can be true or false and their relationships.

**Propositions:** Statements or assertions that express a truth value. Often consist of a predicate (KISS) and one or more arguments (JOHN, MARY)

**Recall:** A metric in AI that measures the proportion of actual positive cases that were correctly identified by the model.

**Reinforcement Learning:** A type of machine learning where agents learn by interacting with an environment and receiving feedback in the form of rewards or punishments. Taken from the psychological notion of *Operant Conditioning*.

**Singularity:** More specifically technological singularity. A hypothetical point in the future where artificial intelligence surpasses human intelligence, leading to unpredictable and uncontrollable societal changes.

**Strong AI:** A theoretical form of artificial intelligence that possesses general intelligence and can perform any intellectual task a human can, including reasoning, understanding, and learning across a broad range of topics. Opposite of *Weak AI*.

**Supervised Learning:** A type of machine learning where models are trained using labelled data to make predictions. The labelled data is compared with the predicted output to determine the performance. Opposite of *Unsupervised Learning*.

**Symbol grounding problem:** Challenge in cognitive science and AI of how symbols (such as words or data) obtain meaning, particularly how abstract symbols can be connected to real-world objects or experiences without relying on other symbols.

**Symbolic AI:** An approach to AI that emphasizes symbolic reasoning and rule-based systems. Always gives correct results, but very difficult to scale up. Also called *Good Old-Fashioned AI*.

**Symbolic systems:** Cognitive models that represent information through symbols and formal rules.

**Theory-driven:** Approaches that start with a theoretical framework or hypothesis to guide the analysis of data. Opposite of *Data-driven*.

**Training:** The process of teaching a machine learning model to recognize patterns in data by adjusting its parameters. In the training phase the parameters of the model are adjusted, and the final settings of these parameters are tested in the testing phase.

**Transformer models:** A type of deep learning model particularly effective for natural language processing tasks, using mechanisms like attention for sequence processing.

**Turing test:** Also called the imitation game. Test proposed by Alan Turing to determine if a machine can exhibit intelligent behaviour indistinguishable from that of a human. If human judges cannot distinguish whether they are dealing with a human or a machine, the machine passed the Turing test.

**Unsupervised Learning:** A type of machine learning where models find patterns in data without labelled examples. The opposite of *Supervised learning*.

**Weak AI:** AI systems that are specialized in narrow tasks, capable of performing specific functions such as language translation or image recognition, but lacking general intelligence or self-awareness. Opposite of *Strong AI*.

**Weights:** Parameters in a neural network that determine the strength of the connections between nodes and are adjusted during the training of the network, for instance through *backpropagation*.

**Word embeddings:** Representations of words as vectors in continuous space, capturing their meanings based on context. See also *distributional semantics*.

# NOTES

## CHAPTER 1

1 For further background and recommended readings, please see Anderson (2020), Boden (2016), Eysenck & Keane (2020) and Warwick (2013).

2 There are exceptions, such as the sea star, sea cucumber, coral, and the Portuguese Man-O-War that happen to not have a brain per se.

3 For species with very simple or microscopic body plans, the presence and structure of a nervous system can be difficult to ascertain.

4 Minsky (1988).

5 Menary (2010). Note that the idea of an extended mind becomes quite meaningful when considering how artificial intelligence may complement our cognitive processes.

6 Russel & Norvig (2020).

7 https://www.bbc.com/news/blogs-magazine-monitor-35428300

8 McCarthy et al. (1955).

9 See also Chapter 5.

10 Miller (2003).

11 These words that contain so many different meanings all packed into them are aptly called "suitcase words" (Minsky, 2006).

12 Maslow (1966).

13 Neuroscientist David Marr (1982) proposed that complex information processing systems should be analysed at three different levels: the computational, algorithmic and implementational level. This distinction is now commonly known as Marr's tri-level hypothesis.

14 The quote can be loosely traced back to De Vaucanson's mechanical ducks in the 17th century (https://en.wikipedia.org/wiki/Duck_test).

15 See Chapter 8.

## CHAPTER 2

1 For further background and recommended reading, please see Bennett (2023); Hunt (2010); Lee (2020).

2 Wissler (1901).

3 He also coined the notions "nature" and "nurture" for which he never really received credit.

4 https://stanfordbinettest.com/quiz/full-quiz

5 Wechsler Adult Intelligence Scale, Fifth Edition (www.pearsonassessments.com).

6 Nisbett et al. (2012).

7 McDaniel (2005).

8 Flynn (2013).

9 Inoue & Matsuzawa (2007).

10 Adams (1979).

11 Franklin & Graesser (1997).

12 Plenary talk John von Neumann (1948).

13 John McCarthy, one of the Dartmouth participants dubbed it "the AI Effect" (Haenlein & Kaplan, 2019).

14 Simon & Newell (1958).

15 Minsky (1988).

16 Moravec (1988).

17 Turing (1950).

18 Both the 2012 and 2014 milestones are highly contested and do not officially constitute "passing" the Turing Test.

19 Chalmers (2010).

## CHAPTER 3

1 For background literature and further recommended readings, please see Chater (2018); Christian & Griffiths (2016); Gigerenzer (2008); Kahneman (2011), and Summerfield (2022).

2 Chen et al. (1997).

3 Gillan et al. (1981).

4 Kintsch (1998).

5 Rumelhart & Ortony (1977).

6 Specifically, AI would tackle a problem like this using algorithms such as Breadth-First Search (BFS) or Depth-First Search (DFS).

7 For instance, WordNet was one of the computational components of IBM Watson.

8 Lenat (1995).

9 Doug Lenat, "What AI Can Learn from Romeo & Juliet," *Forbes*, July 3, 2019, https://www.forbes.com/sites/cognitiveworld/2019/07/03/what-ai-can-learn-from-romeo--juliet/.

10 Newell & Simon (1976, p. 116).

11 *Dreyfus* (1979, p. 157).

12 Zadeh (1965).

13 Kahneman (2011).

14 Gigerenzer (2008).

15 Chater (2018).

## CHAPTER 4

1 For background literature, or further recommended readings, please see Gazzaniga (2009); Kelleher (2019); Krohn et al. (2019); Swaab (2019); and Thamm et al. (2020).

2 Swaab (2019).

3 Admittedly, neurons use graded potentials, firing rates, and temporal patterns but the basic idea holds.

4 Gazzaniga (2009).

5 Greenfield (2008).

6 Schoenemann et al. (2005).

7 Shapson-Coe et al. (2024).

8 Rosenblatt called these hidden layers "association units". The term "hidden layer" was coined in 1974 by Paul Werbos.

9 While artificial neural networks don't have inherent noise like biological neurons, introducing noise during training can actually help them perform better by mimicking some aspects of biological learning.

10 Quillian (1963).

11 Rosch et al. (1976).

12 Louwerse (2021).

## CHAPTER 5

1 For background literature and further recommended reading, please see Alpaydin (2020); Hasselgrove (2016); Gross (2014).

2 Hebb (1949).

3 More formally known as Hebb's Rule or Cell Assembly Theory.

4 Phelps et al. (2022).

5 Cooper et al. (2001).

6 https://www.apa.org/monitor/julaug02/eminent

7 Mitchell(1997).

8 Christian & Griffiths (2016).

9 Alpaydin (2020).

10 Bengio et al. (2017).

11 In all fairness, this example could also be solved by the early perceptron. But as an illustration it suffices.

12 Rumelhart & McClelland (1986).

13 Bengio et al. (2017).

## CHAPTER 6

1 For background literature and further recommended readings, please see Aitchinson (2011); Harley (2013), Landauer et al. (2007) and Louwerse (2021).

2 Chomsky (1972).

3 Hockett (1960).

4 Firth (1957).

5 It is noteworthy this backlash is found in 1980 and in then late 1990s, both times during which society became disappointed with the accomplishments in AI, the so-called AI winters.

6 Searle (1980).

7 Harnad (1990).

8 Weizenbaum (1976).

9 Louwerse (2021).

10 Actually word tokens, but I will leave that aside for now.

11 Christiansen & Chater (2022).

12 Marjieh et al. (2024).

13 Redington, Chater, & Finch (1998).

14 Dingemanse et al. (2015).

## CHAPTER 7

1 For background literature and further recommend readings, please see Enns (2004), Kelleher (2019) and Krohn et al. (2019).

2 Kim et al. (2021).

3 Haenssle, et al. (2018).

4 Morton & Johnson (1991).

5 Kamps et al. (2020).

6 Jenkins et al. (2018).

7 Caharel et al. (2014).

8 What is called the "Thatcher illusion".

9 Weldon, Taubert, Smith, & Parr (2013).

10 Or more specifically a Hidden Markov Model.

11 Bengio, et al. (2017).

12 *Amen, Brother* by The Winstons for instance, sampled in over 6,000 songs.

## CHAPTER 8

1 For background literature and for recommended readings please see Harari (2024); Jones (2022); Kurzweil (2024) and Shneiderman (2022).

2 But more recently we timidly start asking the question whether we are smart enough to know how smart animals are (De Waal, 2016).

3 Berlin artist uses 99 phones to trick Google into traffic jam alert. *The Guardian*, 3 February 2020.

4 2.5 petabytes (1 petabyte = 1,000 terabytes) GPT-3 was trained on hundreds of billions of word tokens (approximately 570 gigabytes of text).

5 https://www.forbes.com/sites/bernardmarr/2018/05/21/how-much-data-do-we-create-every-day-the-mind-blowing-stats-everyone-should-read/

6 As it was in the 1960s and the 1980s.

7 Preskill (2023).

8 After The Police, *Every breath you take*.

9 Keynes (1930).

10 New York Times March 22, 1876.

11 New York Times, November 7 1877.

12 https://arxiv.org/pdf/1911.00650

13 Kasparov (2017).

14 Jones (2017).

# REFERENCES

Adams, D. (1979). *The hitchhiker's guide to the galaxy*. Pan Books.

Aitchison, J. (2011). *The articulate mammal: An introduction to psycholinguistics*. Routledge.

Alpaydin, E. (2020). *Introduction to machine learning*. MIT press.

Anderson, J. R. (2020). *Cognitive psychology and its implications*. Macmillan.

Bengio, Y., Goodfellow, I., & Courville, A. (2017). *Deep learning*. MIT press.

Bennett, M. (2023). *A brief history of intelligence: Why the evolution of the brain holds the key to the future of AI*. William Collins.

Boden, M. A. (2016). *AI: Its nature and future*. Oxford University Press.

Caharel, S., Ramon, M., & Rossion, B. (2014). Face familiarity decisions take 200 msec in the human brain: Electrophysiological evidence from a go/no-go speeded task. *Journal of Cognitive Neuroscience, 26*(1), 81–95.

Chalmers, D. J. (2010). The singularity: A philosophical analysis. *Journal of Consciousness Studies, 17*, 7–65.

Chater, N. (2018). *The mind is flat: The illusion of mental depth and the improvised mind*. Penguin.

Chen, Z., Sanchez, R. P., & Campbell, T. (1997). From beyond to within their grasp: The rudiments of analogical problem solving in 10-and 13-month-olds. *Developmental Psychology, 33*(5), 790–801.

Chomsky, N. (1972). *Studies on semantics in generative grammar*. Mouton de Gruyter.

Christian, B., & Griffiths, T. (2016). *Algorithms to live by: The computer science of human decisions*. Macmillan.

Christiansen, M. H., & Chater, N. (2022). *The language game: How improvisation created language and changed the world*. Random House.

Cooper, J. O., Heron, T. E., & Heward, W. L. (2001). *Applied behavior analysis*. Pearson.

De Waal, F. (2016). *Are we smart enough to know how smart animals are?* WW Norton & Company.

Dingemanse, M., Blasi, D. E., Lupyan, G., Christiansen, M. H., & Monaghan, P. (2015). Arbitrariness, iconicity, and systematicity in language. *Trends in Cognitive Sciences, 19*(10), 603–615.

Dreyfus, H. (1979). *What computers still can't do*. MIT Press.

Enns, J. T. (2004). *The thinking eye, the seeing brain: Explorations in visualcognition*. Norton.

Eysenck, M. W., & Keane, M. T. (2020). *Cognitive psychology: A student's handbook*. Psychology press.

Finch, S., & Chater, N. (1992). Bootstrapping syntactic categories. In *Proceedings of the Annual Meeting of the Cognitive Science Society, 14*, 820–825.

Firth, J. R. (1957). *Papers in linguistics, 1934–1951*. Oxford University Press.

Flynn, J. R. (2013). The "Flynn effect" and Flynn's paradox. *Intelligence, 41*(6), 851–857.

Franklin, S., & Graesser, A. (1997). Is it an agent, or just a program?: A taxonomy for autonomous agents. In *Proceedings of the Third International Workshop on Agent Theories, Architectures, and Languages* (pp. 21–35). Springer-Verlag.

Gazzaniga, M. (2009). *Human: The science behind what makes your brain unique*. Harper Collins.

Gigerenzer, G. (2008). *Gut feelings: Short cuts to better decision making*. Penguin.

Gillan, D. J., Premack, D., & Woodruff, G. (1981). Reasoning in the chimpanzee: I. Analogical reasoning. *Journal of Experimental Psychology: Animal Behavior Processes, 7*(1), 1–17.

Grace, K., Salvatier, J., Dafoe, A., Zhang, B., & Evans, O. (2018). When will AI exceed human performance? Evidence from AI experts. *Journal of Artificial Intelligence Research, 62*, 729–754.

Greenfield, S. A. (2008). *The human brain: A guided tour*. Basic Books.

Haenlein, M. & Kaplan, A. (2019). A brief history of artificial intelligence: On the past, present, and future of artificial intelligence. *California Management Review, 61*(4), 5–14.

Haenssle, H. A., Fink, C., Schneiderbauer, R., Toberer, F., Buhl, T., Blum, A., ... & Zalaudek, I. (2018). Man against machine: diagnostic performance of a deep learning convolutional neural network for dermoscopic melanoma recognition in comparison to 58 dermatologists. *Annals of Oncology*, 29(8), 1836–1842.

Harari, Y. N. (2024). *Nexus: A brief history of information networks from the Stone Age to AI.* Signal.

Harley, T. A. (2013). *The psychology of language: From data to theory.* Psychology press.

Harnad, S. (1990). The symbol grounding problem. *Physica D: Nonlinear Phenomena*, 42(1–3), 335–346.

Haselgrove, M. (2016). *Learning: A very short introduction.* Oxford University Press.

Hockett, C. F. (1960). *A course in modern linguistics.* Macmillan.

Hunt, E. (2010). *Human intelligence.* Cambridge University Press.

Inoue, S., & Matsuzawa, T. (2007). Working memory of numerals in chimpanzees. *Current Biology*, 17(23), R1004-R1005.

Jenkins, R., Dowsett, A. J., & Burton, A. M. (2018). How many faces do people know?. *Proceedings of the Royal Society B*, 285(1888), 20181319.

Jones, H. (2022). *When AI rules the world: China, the US, and the race to control a smart planet.* Bombardier Books.

Jones, M. N. (Ed.). (2017). *Big data in cognitive science.* Routledge.

Kahneman, D. (2011). *Thinking, fast and slow.* Farrar, Straus and Giroux.

Kamps, F. S., Hendrix, C. L., Brennan, P. A., & Dilks, D. D. (2020). Connectivity at the origins of domain specificity in the cortical face and place networks. *Proceedings of the National Academy of Sciences*, 117(11), 6163–6169.

Kasparov, G. (2017). *Deep thinking: Where machine intelligence ends and human creativity begins.* Hachette.

Kelleher, J. D. (2019). *Deep learning.* MIT press.

Keynes, J. M. (1930). Economic possibilities for our grandchildren. In *Essays in persuasion* (pp. 321–332). London: Palgrave Macmillan UK.

Kim, U. S., Mahroo, O. A., Mollon, J. D., & Yu-Wai-Man, P. (2021). Retinal ganglion cells—diversity of cell types and clinical relevance. *Frontiers in Neurology*, 12, 661938.

Kintsch, W. (1998). *Comprehension: A paradigm for cognition.* Cambridge University Press.

Krohn, J., Beyleveld, G., & Bassens, A. (2019). *Deep learning illustrated: A visual, interactive guide to artificial intelligence.* Addison-Wesley Professional.

Kurzweil, R. (2024). *The singularity is nearer: When we merge with AI.* Random House.

Landauer, T. K., McNamara, D. S., Dennis, S., & Kintsch, W. (Eds.). (2007). *Handbook of latent semantic analysis.* Psychology Press.

Lee, D. (2020). *Birth of intelligence: From RNA to artificial intelligence.* Oxford University Press.

Lenat, D.B. (1995). Cyc: A large-scale investment in knowledge infrastructure. *Communications of the ACM, 38,* 33–38.

Louwerse, M. (2021). *Keeping those words in mind: How language creates meaning.* Rowman & Littlefield.

Marjieh, R., Sucholutsky, I., van Rijn, P., Jacoby, N., & Griffiths, T. L. (2024). Large language models predict human sensory judgments across six modalities. *Scientific Reports, 14*(1), 21445.

Marr, B. (2024). *Generative AI in practice: 100+ amazing ways Generative Artificial Intelligence is changing business and society.* Wiley.

Marr, D. (1982). *Vision: A computational investigation into the human representation and processing of visual information.* WH Freeman.

Maslow, A. H. (1966) *The psychology of science.* Joanna Cotler Books.

McCarthy, J., Minsky, M.L., Rochester, N., & Shannon, C.E. (1955). *A proposal for the Dartmouth summer research project on artificial intelligence.*

McDaniel, M. A. (2005). Big-brained people are smarter: A meta-analysis of the relationship between in vivo brain volume and intelligence. *Intelligence, 33*(4), 337–346.

Menary, R. (2010). *The extended mind.* MIT Press.

Miller, G. A. (2003). The cognitive revolution: A historical perspective. *Trends in Cognitive Sciences, 7*(3), 141–144.

Minsky, M. (1988). *The society of mind.* Simon and Schuster.

Minsky, M. (2007). *The emotion machine: Commonsense thinking, artificial intelligence, and the future of the human mind.* Simon and Schuster.

Mitchell, T. (1997). *Machine learning.* McGraw Hill.

Moravec, H. H. (1988). *Mind children.* Harvard University Press.

Morton, J., & Johnson, M. H. (1991). CONSPEC and CONLERN: A two-process theory of infant face recognition. *Psychological Review, 98*(2), 164–181.

Nisbett, R.E., Aronson, J., Blair, C., Dickens, W., Flynn, J.R., Halpern, D.F., & Turkheimer E. (2012). Intelligence: New findings and theoretical developments. *American Psychologist, 67*(2), 130–159.

Phelps, E. A., Gazzaniga, M. S., & Berkman, E. T. (2022). *Psychological science.* WW Norton.

Preskill, J. (2023). Quantum computing 40 years later. In *Feynman Lectures on Computation* (pp. 193–244). CRC Press.

Quillian, R. (1963). *A notation for representing conceptual information: An application to semantics and mechanical English paraphrasing.* SP-1395, System Development Corporation, Santa Monica.

Redington, M., Chater, N., & Finch, S. (1998). Distributional information: A powerful cue for acquiring syntactic categories. *Cognitive Science, 22*(4), 425–469.

Rosch, E., Simpson, C., & Miller, R. S. (1976). Structural bases of typicality effects. *Journal of Experimental Psychology: Human Perception and Performance, 2*(4), 491–502.

Rumelhart, D. E., & McClelland, J. L. (1986). *Parallel distributed processing: Exploration in the microstructure of the cognition.* MIT Press.

Rumelhart, D. E., & Ortony, A. (1977). The representation of knowledge in memory. In *Schooling and the acquisition of knowledge* (pp. 99–135). Erlbaum.

Russell, S. J., & Norvig, P. (2016). *Artificial intelligence: A modern approach.* Pearson.

Schoenemann, P.T., Sheehan, M. J., & Glotzer, L. D. (2005). Prefrontal white matter volume is disproportionately larger in humans than in other primates. *Nature Neuroscience, 8*(2), 242–252.

Searle, J. R. (1980) Minds, brains, and programs. *Behavioral and Brain Sciences, 3*(3): 417–457

Shapson-Coe, A., Januszewski, M., Berger, D. R., Pope, A., Wu, Y., Blakely, T., . . . & Lichtman, J. W. (2024). A petavoxel fragment of human cerebral cortex reconstructed at nanoscale resolution. *Science, 384*(6696), eadk4858.

Shneiderman, B. (2022). *Human-centered AI.* Oxford University Press.

Simon, H. A., & Newell, A. (1958). Heuristic problem solving: The next advance in operations research. *Operations Research, 6*(1), 1–10.

Simon, H. A., & Newell, A. (1976). Computer science as empirical inquiry: Symbols and search. *Communications of the ACM, 19*(3), 113–126.

Summerfield, C. (2022). *Natural General Intelligence: How understanding the brain can help us build AI.* Oxford university press.

Swaab, D. (2019). *Our creative brains.* Atlas Contact.

Thamm, A., Gramlich, M., & Borek, A. (2020). *The ultimate data and AI guide: 150 FAQs about artificial intelligence, machine learning and data.* Data AI Press.

Thompson, P. (1980). Margaret Thatcher: A new illusion. *Perception, 9*(4): 483–484.

Tibbetts, E. A., Agudelo, J., Pandit, S., & Riojas, J. (2019). Transitive inference in Polistes paper wasps. *Biology Letters, 15*(5), 20190015.

Turing, A. M. (1950). Computing machinery and intelligence. *Mind*, 59(236), 433–460.

Wade, N., & Swanston, M. (2013). *Visual perception: An introduction.* Psychology Press.

Warwick, K. (2013). *Artificial intelligence: The basics.* Routledge.

Weizenbaum, J. (1976). *Computer power and human reason: From judgment to calculation.* Freeman and Company.

Weldon, K. B., Taubert, J., Smith, C. L., & Parr, L. A. (2013). How the Thatcher illusion reveals evolutionary differences in the face processing of primates. *Animal Cognition*, 16(5), 691–700.

Wissler, C. (1901). The correlation of mental and physical tests. *Psychological Review*, 16, 1–62.

Zadeh, L. A. (1965). Information and control. *Fuzzy sets*, 8(3), 338–353.

# INDEX

For Product Safety Concerns and Information please contact our EU
representative  GPSR@taylorandfrancis.com
Taylor & Francis Verlag GmbH, Kaufingerstraße 24, 80331 München, Germany

www.ingramcontent.com/pod-product-compliance
Lightning Source LLC
Chambersburg PA
CBHW070944050326
40689CB00014B/3335